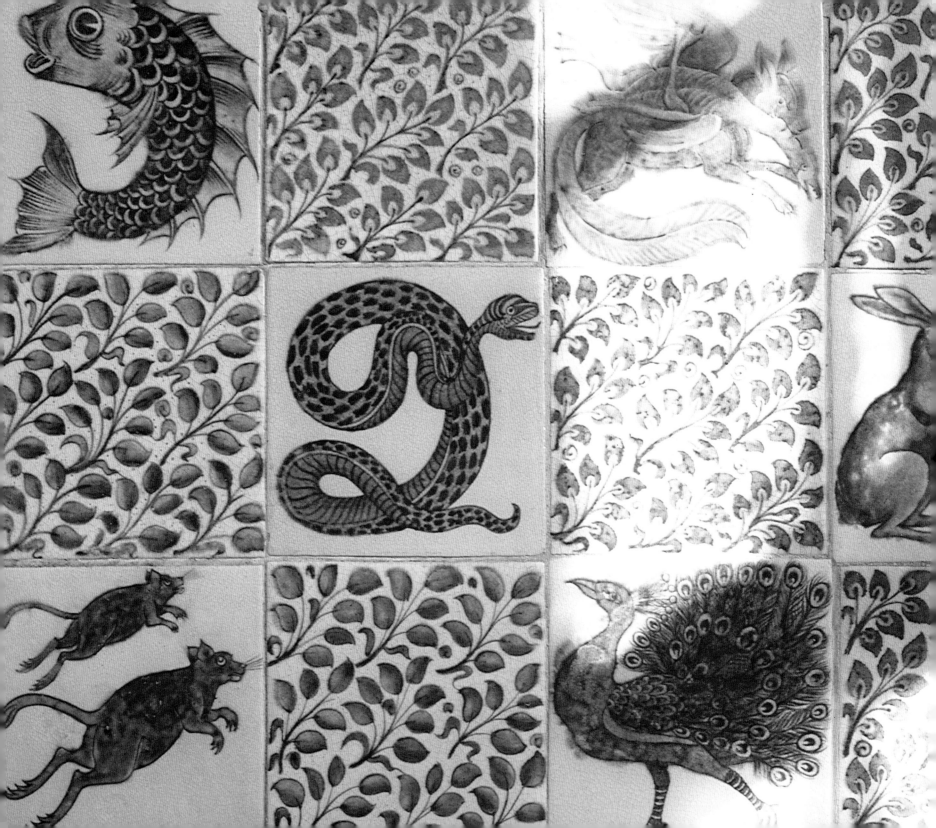

AN ALBUM OF
CURIOUS
HOUSES

PHOTOGRAPHED AND
DESCRIBED BY
LUCINDA LAMBTON

AN ALBUM OF

CURIOUS HOUSES

PHOTOGRAPHED & DESCRIBED BY

LUCINDA LAMBTON

CHATTO & WINDUS
LONDON

Published in 1988 by

CHATTO & WINDUS LTD

30 Bedford Square

London WC1B 3SG

A CIP catalogue record for this book is available from the British Library.

ISBN 0 7011 3119 5

Text and photographs

copyright © Lucinda Lambton

Design by Trickett and Webb

Colour originated and printed by

Butler and Tanner Ltd,

Frome, Somerset

Photoset by Rowland Phototypesetting Ltd,

Bury St Edmunds, Suffolk

Endpapers: Titles by William de Morgan (1906) at 8 Addison Road, London
Half-title and page 160: Mice crawling through the walls of Cardiff Castle
Frontispiece: The Triangular Lodge, Northamptonshire
Title page: Detail of the Triangular Lodge

CONTENTS

FOR JONATHAN GILI

FOREWORD

THIS BOOK HAS BEEN WRITTEN AND THE PHOTOGRAPHS HAVE BEEN TAKEN TO ACCLAIM AND APPLAUD A COLLECTION OF HOUSES AND THEIR BUILDERS. THEY ARE ALL REMARKABLE architectural flights of fancy: some of them are beautiful, a few are hideous, but all have been chosen for their high spirited originality and exuberance, with the greatest admiration for their architects, designers and craftsmen.

An underwater smoking room built at the turn of the century; a timber-framed house perched in the branches of a lime tree for over three hundred years; a giant glass and tubular bird commissioned by a lady botanist as her retirement home in 1981; the miniature Moorish pavilion Amon Henry Wilds built for himself in Brighton in 1827; the sensationally strange Mount Stuart, built by the Marquis of Bute on the Island of Bute in 1890; and the Gothic/Arts and Crafts/post-modern house the artist Graham Ovenden is creating on Bodmin Moor today. The triumph of all these adventurous buildings and their builders must be cheered to the skies.

LUCINDA LAMBTON

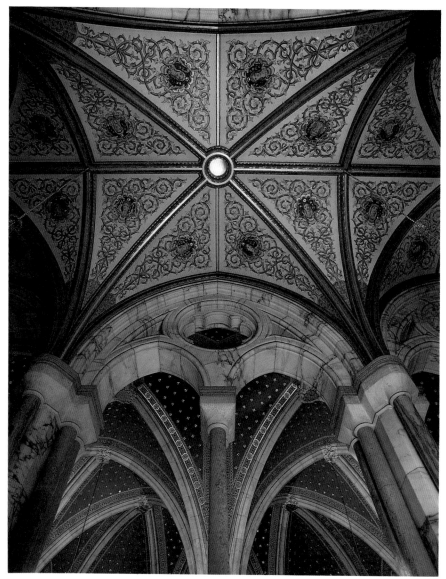

The vaulted hall gallery

Exterior

The drawing room ceiling

Capital of a marble pillar in the drawing room

MOUNT STUART

Isle of Bute

THE FIRST SIGHT OF MOUNT STUART ON THE ISLE OF BUTE IN SCOTLAND MAKES YOU SHOUT WITH DELIGHT: A mixture of Venetian, French and Spanish Gothic, it is so totally unexpected and so very extraordinary. It was rebuilt by the third Marquis of Bute after a fire in 1879. He employed Rowand Anderson as his architect, but he was largely responsible for the house's sumptuous interior himself, meticulously supervising all the artists and artisans for over twenty years.

Lord Bute was a serious and scholarly man of extraordinary abilities, a romantic and a mystic, an astrologer, historian, archaeologist and theologian who wove all his erudition into a passion for building.

From an early age, he had shown little conformity; Sir Herbert Maxwell, in his book *Evening Memories*, wrote of the twenty-one-year-old Lord Bute being encouraged, in vain, to pursue country activities. 'I retain an impression of him shivering in a woodland ride, the ground being covered with snow. He had on his feet a pair of patent leather shoes, and under his arm a gun which he knew not how to handle. I don't think he ever went out shooting again . . . He used to amuse us by coming to the smoking room at night arrayed in a gorgeous flowing robe modelled after the pattern and colour of a saint's mantle as depicted in a stained glass window of the school chapel at Harrow. If I remember it aright it was sky-blue silk lined with violet and enriched with plenty of broad gold lace.'

His obsession with medievalism had flowered at Cardiff with Burges's influence, but at Mount Stuart the schemes were often to his own designs. Burges thought that his mirrored drawing room ceiling, entwined with vines, was 'damnable'!

The great hall at Mount Stuart is sixty feet square and eighty feet high, of sheer soaring splendour, with

Ornate brass door hinges

The drawing room

Bell push and light switch

Views of the Great Hall

gleaming marble and brilliant stained glass, rushing up to the central vault emblazoned with the constellations. A vaulted gallery marches round, with a translucent boss to each vault, surrounded by muses with jewelled stars in their hair. The entire hall shines with the colours of the glass, with the signs of the zodiac and mythological figures and creatures, charging through waves of scarlet, purple and blue. It was all designed by Horatio Walter Lonsdale and executed by Worrall. Mount Stuart is a dazzling example of nineteenth-century eclecticism laced with the bravado of the day. Lord Bute built an immense white marble church of a chapel, which is permanently aglow with the blood red of its clerestory glass, and he and William Frame designed other exhaustingly elaborate ceilings. Most surprising of all is the vaulted, Gothic swimming pool, through which you glide, as if swimming up the aisle of a parish church.

Lord Bute died in 1900, before all the work on the house was carried out, but now, eighty-eight years later, it is being finished. The present Lord and Lady Bute are in the midst of a seven-year programme of conservation and renovation. There were never any plans, so much of the work will have to be conjecture and a lot will be commissioned in the spirit of the house, rather than in slavish imitation. The jambs of the sandstone fireplace in the conservatory were never carved, and they are about to be today, with mice peering out of oak leaves (the family emblem) on one side, with a cat peering over at them from the other.

Lord Bute is active in encouraging a host of young craftsmen all over Scotland: he is involved with companies of furniture makers, stonemasons, wood carvers and textile designers. His firm, the Edinburgh Tapestry Company, has just finished a range of tapestries for PepsiCo with designs by Frank Stella. Three admiring cheers for both Lord Bute and his great-grandfather.

The swimming pool

The chapel

BARLEY SPLATT

Cornwall

BARLEY SPLATT BEATS MOST OTHER MODERN HOUSES BUILT TODAY IN THE BRITISH ISLES INTO A COCKED HAT. To see such richness of materials, with such originality of design, gives sheer satisfaction and complete delight.

It is still being built by the painter Graham Ovenden who moved from London to live on the edge of Bodmin Moor in 1973, having seen an advertisement in *Dalton's Weekly* for a Cornish cottage in a valley with a river and twenty-two acres. Finding it to be particularly isolated, over a tiny fifteenth-century bridge and up a long and tortuous tunnel of a lane, he bought the little house and has been adventurously transforming it ever since. Graham Ovenden is a man of many parts, with all of them working flat out, all of the time. He is an artist, a printmaker and a photographer, a musician and a poet, who has designed and built his own house, and filled it with his vast collection of books, many of which he has written himself.

He has always had a passionate interest in the applied arts of the nineteenth century. John Betjeman was a friend. 'I got from him a particular delight in the Gothic Revival.' Frank Lloyd Wright, with his sense of geometry and artistic unity, is an architect whom Ovenden greatly admires. Both influences bristle out of Barley Splatt, along with another: the totally unexpected but excitingly apparent forms of a Second World War aeroplane engine. Graham Ovenden grew up with his father's plans for aircraft design. Homage is paid to Cornwall with the tower, to both the Cornish round stair towers and the tin mine chimneys, but with all this there is no shadow of a hotch potch in the powerful and definite design and decoration of the house. He admits that 'it borrows, as any piece of architecture does, but Barley Splatt tends to look like Barley Splatt.'

Ovenden has built the house largely himself, cutting the granite from his own fields where he has also picked up many of the stones. For the polychromatic effects he has used marble, granite, stone and Elizabethan brick, claiming that all later bricks are riddled through with little bubbles. 'If I do have a philosophy of Architecture it is integrity to indigenous materials. This is an important part of what architecture is about. On the other hand I am very happy to use any modern construction technique.'

Underneath all its finery, Barley Splatt has a concrete core. 'The problem is how purist you want to be. You notice the tower has drip eaves, not guttering . . . aesthetically it looks much better without guttering, but as you know from the puddle on the stair carpet, such purist considerations have their drawbacks.'

Graham Ovenden is one of the inventors of 'Post Modernism'. 'It was a committee invention.' He gives Charles Jencks all the credit for its publicisation and propaganda, although he would far rather see the style orientated towards the gothic than towards the classical. 'Gothic building is more demanding, the quality of craftsmanship must necessarily be greater. Classicism is cheaper.'

At the time of writing, Barley Splatt is half finished, but there are monumental plans afoot, with towers galore, all with either glass spires or striped 'hats' for roofs. The main body of the house will be a great hall with flying buttresses, and decorated chimney stacks will rear up at every turn. Ovenden often changes his mind as he builds, with the house evolving not unlike a sculpture, as he works away, always with the highest standards of craftsmanship. He plans to design everything eventually, including the wallpapers and all the furniture. 'If one is mad enough to begin something like Barley Splatt, you might as well go the whole hog.'

The colours and contrasts of Barley Splatt

WESTERN PAVILION

Brighton

SOME THREE MILLION VISITORS FLOCK TO BRIGHTON EVERY YEAR. THE TOWN'S POPULARITY RESTS ON THE DELIGHTFUL foundations of Dr Russell's *Dissertation concerning the Use of Sea Water in Diseases of the Glands*. This was published in Latin in 1750 and in English in 1753, and its recommendation of the chalybeate spring at St Ann's Well Gardens brought the first trickle of visitors to the town.

The Prince Regent arrived in 1783 and settled into a modest farmhouse in 1786, while first his stables, with their dome only twenty feet short of the dome of St. Paul's, and then Nash's great Pavilion, were built. But the building boom which transformed the town, doubling the number of houses from 4,000 to 8,000 in elegant squares, terraces and crescents, took place between 1820 and 1830 and it was largely carried out by three architects, Charles Augustus Busby, Amon

Wilds and his son Amon Henry Wilds. Amon Henry Wilds was particularly interesting, in that his building spanned the Regency and Victorian periods of architecture. He was helping his father with Regency Square from 1818 onwards and was designing the cast iron dolphin fountain for the Steine Gardens in 1846.

The most successful and the most charming of all his buildings was the little Western Pavilion which he designed for himself in 1827. Hidden away down a tiny cul-de-sac off the Western Road, it is one of a small group that make up a most elegant exercise in architecture: a 'gothick' house with crocketed pinnacles and tracery galore, a perfect classical terrace with ammonite pilasters (which he often used, as a pun on his name), and this oriental pavilion, with Saracenic arches, minarets and dome. The gothic house was built by his father and Busby, all the rest were built by him, and it is thought he financed the whole scheme. He lived in five out of the ten houses over the years.

Amon Henry Wilds was involved with several oriental plans in Brighton: both 'Oriental Terrace' and 'Oriental Place' as well as three other houses, all of which were built, and two garden schemes which were doomed to terrible failure. In 1825 Henry Phillips, a landscape gardener and botanist, asked Wilds for help in designing a vast steam-heated conservatory, with three bulging onion domes, that he planned to build in the gardens that were to lead out of 'Oriental Place'. It would be called the Athenaeum and was to be large enough to house fully grown palms and other tropical trees, as well as a library, reading room, museum and a school for the sciences and liberal arts. Sadly the money could not be raised and it was never built. But much much worse was to follow, eight years later, in nearby Hove.

In 1832, undeterred by the failure of the Athenaeum, Henry Phillips planned to build yet another and even bigger Moresque conservatory, and to call it the Antheum. It was to have the largest glass dome in the world, 165 feet in diameter and 65 feet high, topped with an ogival cupola and vast enough to span over a lake, set in a landscape of walks, arbors, trees and shrubs. The glass was to be supported by cast iron ribs, rising up to the capital of a central cast iron pillar, on top of which was an observatory and a gallery. Half way through the building work, it was decided to remove the centre post and, fearing that it would all collapse, Wilds resigned. On 29 August 1833 the temporary supports were taken away and a day later the whole structure crashed to the ground. For twenty years the twisted mountain of metal lay where it had landed, where it was inspected with interest by Joseph Paxton in 1850.

ONE OF THE RAREST ROOMS IN ALL ENGLAND IS THE HALL OF 4 MAIDS OF HONOUR ROW. WITH PAINTED panels framed by sumptuous scroll work and *en grisaille* cartouches of the seasons and the arts in faded gold, it is a unique survival in England of a grand rococo room on a tiny scale.

Maids of Honour Row, four elegantly light and well proportioned houses, stands on its own overlooking Richmond Green. They were built between 1724 and 1726 for the ladies-in-waiting to Caroline of Anspach, Princess of Wales, after the Prince had bought the Duke of Ormonde's house nearby as his summer residence. Number 4's most colourful tenant was to be John James Heidegger, manager of the Opera House in the Haymarket and Handel's impresario, and it was he who commissioned the hall paintings from Antonio Jolli between 1744 and 1749.

According to Mrs Delaney, Heidegger was 'the ugliest man that was ever formed'. Hogarth depicted his hideousness with relish, Fielding described him as 'Count Ugli', and Pope wove these physical misfortunes into 'The Dunciad' with the lines,

And lo! her bird (a monster of a fowl
something betwixt a Heidegger and Owl)

Heidegger admitted to his own grotesqueness with cheerful zest, even taking a bet with Lord Chesterfield that no more dreadful face could be found. A formidable female rival was produced but, on Heidegger donning her head dress, the wager was won! Renowned for his knowledge on all things operatic, his wit, easy manner and high spirited entertainments, he became known as the 'Surintendant des Plaisirs d'Angleterre'. His 'Masquerades' at the Opera House gained such scandalous notoriety that a Royal Proclamation was

The wall,
with silent compan

issued to suppress them, with a Middlesex grand jury introducing Heidegger as 'the principal of vice and immorality'. All of which must have been alarming for his father, who was a clergyman in Zurich. Heidegger died in 1749, leaving the house in Maids of Honour Row to his natural daughter Elizabeth Pappet.

The hall paintings were rediscovered in the early 1930s by Mr Edward Croft-Murray, later to become the distinguished Keeper of Prints and Drawings at the British Museum. All the walls were covered with thick brown paint and carriage varnish, antlers were screwed into the dark 'tudorised' panels, and hefty settles, tables and chairs were crammed around the fireplace. This was the all-but-ruinous taste of Charles Garvice, author of dozens of bad romances with such tempting titles as *Diana and Destiny in Cupid's Chains*, *The Earl's Daughter* and *The Coronet of Shame*.

Many months were spent in 1935 restoring the hall, with Edward Croft-Murray tracing the origins of the paintings to three books of prints: Zeiller's and Merian's *Topographia Helvetiae* of 1642 and *Topographia Italiae* of 1688, and J. B. Fischer von Erlach's *Entwurf einer Historischen Architectur* of 1721. On the wall to the left of the fireplace, the Rhine flows past the Cathedral at Basle and then over the falls at Schaffhausen. St. Peter Platz is painted above the cartouche of corn and an unidentified Mediterranean port is in the panel above the fire. On the right, Vesuvius smokes during the eruption of 1631. In the original print, refugees flee over La Ponte Nunciata; here, aesthetes on the Grand Tour survey the sight. On the opposite wall are two Chinese scenes, one of the terrifying chain bridge at Kingtung. The Temple of Sybil at Tivoli is on their right, above burning sticks representing winter. To the right of the door, above the cartouche of a spear, quiver, sword and bow there is a panel of an enormous rock arch, whereabouts unknown.

The first clue as to who had painted the panels came with the discovery of the score of an aria 'Per Pieta bell Idol Mio', which is entwined with a golden rose over a door. This was composed by the infamous Conte de St Germain for his opera *L'Inconstanza Delusa* which was staged by Heidegger in 1745, when his scene painter was known to be Antonio Jolli, pupil of Pannini and contemporary and imitator of Canaletto. The Conte was a fanciful fraud who, as a musician, alchemist and magician, was the toast of the Royal Court of France. He was an intimate of Madame de Pompadour, prancing attendance in diamonds, black velvet and a sky blue peruke. Horace Walpole described him as 'odd . . . he sings and plays the violin wonderfully, is mad and not very sensible.'

Antonio Jolli was first heard of in England in 1744, as the scene painter for the opera *Rosalinda* at the King's Theatre in London. As well as theatrical work, he produced architectural capricci in the style of his master Pannini and various topographical scenes of both Italy and England for houses all over the country. Four of his scenes of Rome were recorded in the Fonthill sale of 1807. He left England in 1750, was elected a member of the Venetian Academy in 1755 and, by 1762, was living in Naples, where Sir William Hamilton bought several of his paintings. His work at 4 Maids of Honour Row is exceptionally fine and painted as it is, covering the walls from floor to ceiling, it is quite overwhelming.

A tree at Basle Cathedral by the Rhine

ELVEDEN

Suffolk

ADMIRAL LORD KEPPLE ONCE LIVED IN THE ORIGINAL EIGHTEENTH-CENTURY HOUSE AT ELVEDEN. IT IS said that he left the library open to the skies and laid planks on the floor so that he could enjoy the sensation of walking the deck until his dying day. In 1748, when he was only twenty-five years old, he had been sent on a mission to sign a treaty with the Dey of Algiers who, enraged and insulted at his youthfulness complained 'that the king of Great Britain should have sent a beardless boy to treat'. Kepple's reply brought threats of instant execution: 'Had my master supposed that wisdom was measured by the length of the beard, he would have sent your deyship a he-goat.'

His rather plain, red brick house was bought in 1863 and virtually rebuilt by the Maharajah Duleep Singh, who had been disgracefully deposed by the English when they annexed the Punjab in 1848, when he was only five years old. He had come to England when he was fifteen and was immediately befriended by Queen Victoria, who was intrigued by the idea of showing him the Koh-i-noor diamond which had been virtually stolen off his arm (he had worn it on an enamelled armlet) ten years before. The scene must have been an extraordinary one: the jewel, now reduced to half its size by European chisellers, was brought from the Tower by Beefeaters, in full regalia, to the White Drawing Room in Buckingham Palace where Winterhalter was painting the young Maharajah. For a full quarter of an hour Duleep Singh gazed at the stone, turning it over and over in his hand; and then, with terrifying poise, he walked over to the Queen and put it into her hand, with the words, 'It is to me, Ma'am, the greatest pleasure thus to have the opportunity, as a loyal subject, of myself tendering to my Sovereign the Koh-i-noor!'

Such elegance of mind and manner appears to have

been eroded as Duleep Singh developed the life of an affluent and obese sporting squire (there are photographs of his immense form in tweeds) on his East India Company pension of between £40,000 and £50,000. He bought the estate at Elveden principally for the shoot and could proudly boast of such vile seasonal 'bags' as 9,600 pheasants and 75,000 rabbits. The house was given an Italianate and balustraded façade by John Norton and a gaudily painted Indian drawing room which, along with the romance of the Maharajah's residency, was undoubtedly the inspiration for the glorious marble Indian Hall that was to be built in 1903.

The Indian Hall

Duleep Singh had died in Paris in 1893, and Elveden was bought by Lord Iveagh who transformed the house into a palace of Edwardian opulence. He commissioned first William Young, then his son Clyde Young, as architects. For the work on the Indian Hall they were to be advised by Sir Caspar Purdon Clerk, the director of

the Victoria and Albert Museum and an architect who had worked in Teheran. He was determined on a very meticulous course of authenticity of detail at Elveden. He wanted it to show the best examples of Moghul architecture in England, and he succeeded: the hall is like a great, living pattern book, with examples of both Hindu and Islamic styles accurately and intricately represented, and all together in one room. The pillars alone are 1,000 years apart in terms of style.

The hall cost £70,000, and was part of the rebuilding, yet again, of Elveden. It was still red brick and, now, rather lumpen Edwardian outside, but inside one of the most sumptuous houses of its day. Augustus Hare described it as 'appallingly luxurious' in 1895, and Chips Channon wrote that he loved 'its calm, its luxurious Edwardian atmosphere' in 1934, although he grumbled that all fifty of the servants had gone to bed when he arrived hungry and cold one night and was unable to get anything to eat. The guests had tea in the Indian Hall after shooting and assembled there after dinner, with Casano's band playing away in the gallery.

Elizabeth, Countess of Fingall, who often stayed at Elveden, thought that hers must have been the coldest room in England and, although there are two fireplaces, she writes in her memoirs *Seventy Years Young* of only one being lit. Edward VII was sometimes a fellow guest, 'when etiquette and courtesy had to be observed, a good many of us froze.' She once danced an Irish jig for the King in the hall (the floor was sprung with buffers); 'I had to take off my skirt and dance in my petticoats, the full elaborate petticoats of those days; and I must have a partner so I seized hold of Sir Frank Lascelles, who was the ambassador to Berlin, and made him stand opposite me. Not knowing the steps of the jig, he could only shuffle his feet and move as I told him. The King laughed a lot but I think it was the spectacle of my partner that amused him most.'

Her bedroom at Elveden was separated from the King's suite by double doors and, unwillingly, she heard many a state secret during his discussions with Balfour. When the King of Portugal was staying in the rooms, only weeks before his assassination, they struck up cheerful yelling conversations over their breakfast trays. 'We were great friends . . . He was a great gentleman and such a jolly fellow.' Chips Channon stayed in the suite of rooms and had a humiliating accident: 'in the wee sma' hours . . . I somehow smashed the royal chamber pot.'

In 1984 there was a grand sale of furniture at Elveden and the great hall now stands empty, as Lady Fingall described it, 'made for the Indian suns, down amid the cold marshes of Suffolk'.

The Indian Hall and its mirrored and marbled details

THE NEW HOUSE

Kent

A HOST OF SURPRISES AWAIT THE FIRST-TIME VISITOR TO THE NEW HOUSE NEAR TUNBRIDGE WELLS, the startling originality of its design, the choice and use of materials with their variety of textures and colours and, above all, the discovery that it is beautifully built, with a satisfying and careful attention to detail, both inside and out.

The entrance front

It was designed between 1983 and 1986 by John Outram who was commissioned to design a modern house that was not an historical pastiche. It was built for an industrialist who is concerned that industry has a bad name, and he was particularly pleased to be able to build a house made up of so many industrial components – steel framing, concrete cladding and asbestos roof.

The plans took five years to develop, going through all manner of construction systems and designs. John Outram can remember, at one stage, being told,

'"John, I would like it to be like a stone," . . . He wanted it to be original but very quiet and mute, neither demonstrative nor rhetorical . . . it is less mute than was probably expected but at the same time it doesn't say things that are all that intelligible . . . you couldn't say that it is Baroque or Elizabethan.' It is magnificently situated, crowning a ridge, high over Kent, on the site of a vast Victorian mansion which was demolished in 1952. The ruin of a conservatory remained and has been cleverly and sumptuously transformed into an open air room with a black and white marble floor and concrete pillars clad in brick.

It was bought with an estate of 600 acres for a deer park and stocked with over 1,000 creatures. One of the main concerns for the house was to have windows big enough to embrace the views. 'So the walls disappeared,' says John Outram, 'and they became columns.' Each one is hollow, filled with a steel frame and the

The north and the south-western fronts

The conservatory, detail of doors and the front hall

service piping and each one is covered with John Outram's 'fancy concrete' mixtures. Marble and stone were considered, but marble was too expensive and also too fragile. Both would have had to be cut so thin, which the joins at the corners would have revealed, and there would have been none of the satisfying solidity that was wanted. Concrete, on the other hand, gives the impression of great 'blocks' and there are four varieties of aggregate round every pillar: pebble, limestone, lacquered black marble 'capitals' and John Outram's invention, 'Blitzcrete', a mixture of crushed brick and rubble, which has been ground off and polished up to expose the great chips of terracotta.

A cornice of green concrete marches round overall, with deeply cut sloping grooves, intersected by the gleaming 'capitals' that are either floodlights or water-spouts for overflowing gutters.

Inside the house there is the happiest harmony of craftsmanship and colour, with wooden floors, walls and vaulted ceilings and veneered and inlaid surfaces in pale pinks, greens, mauves and greys.

The hall shines brightest of all, with polished walls of 'stucco lustro' banded with burr elm and aluminium, inlaid trellis-work doors and the travertine floor laid out so as to look like a base of a Corinthian column. 'Stucco lustro' is crushed marble and lime put on with a hot trowel, then mottled with a sponge, left to dry and beeswaxed to a lustrous shine some months later.

The doors are of avodire wood, inlaid with a trellis-work of 2,500 strips of pale and dark grey dyed syca-more, all giving the strangely soft effect of moleskin.

With the views outside and the airiness within, the New House has an atmosphere through which you float with delight, constantly aware that everything around you has been so well made. It is all of a perfect piece which gives a feeling of great satisfaction and cosiness.

THE OAK LODGE
Buckinghamshire

A T THE END OF ONE OF THE DRIVES TO HALL BARN, BEACONSFIELD, THE MID-SEVENTEENTH-CENTURY HOUSE designed and built by the poet and politician Edmund Waller, stands the Oak Lodge. The cladding has rotted and been restored over the years, with its carvings constantly evolving, culminating in the 1980s in a triumphant restoration by Lord Burnham, the owner of Hall Barn, and Colin Mantripp, woodcarver.

Edmund Waller was born in 1605 and entered Parliament when he was only sixteen years old. He eased his way through kings and Commonwealth, writing panegyrics to Charles I, Cromwell and Charles II. He was related to the Lord Protector through his mother who was a zealous Royalist. Dr Johnson gives a delightful account of Cromwell arguing with Mrs Waller: 'he would throw a napkin at her and say he would not dispute with his aunt'.

Waller rebuilt Hall Barn in 1651 and laid out the magnificent gardens which survive to this day with their temples, obelisks and rampant topiaries. Lord Percival wrote of visiting the gardens in 1724: 'a woman in full health cannot walk them all, for which reason my wife was carry'd in a Windsor chair like those at Versailles, by which means she lost nothing worth seeing'.

The house has had uncomfortable additions, but Lord Burnham has recently restored it to Waller's seventeenth-century glory. Once again it is the elegant 'London Box', as described by Lord Percival. In 1980 Oak Lodge was in a sorry state of disrepair: some restoration had been done in the 1970s but with a machine wielded by an amateur, 'a chap from the Gas Board', and a great many of the carvings were rotten with the wood crumbling away like cork. But one day, by a stroke of good luck, its future was assured.

Newly established as a woodcarver, Colin Mantripp

A confection of carving

Lord Burnham

was looking at the carvings and yearning to do work on them when he 'fell into conversation with a gentleman who had stopped his car'. It was Lord Burnham, who had been searching for someone who could do that very work. It was started within days, and within weeks Mantripp discovered that his great great great uncle had done much of the carving on Oak Lodge in the early 1900s. He had inherited his tools from this uncle, the same ones that were now sculpting away on the same building some eighty years later.

It took four years to restore, ending up as it always was meant to be, a rich confection of carvings of all ages: top rails from James II chairs decorate the porch, with printing blocks marching up and down the gable, and many of the carvings on the façade are known to be from a church that was dismantled in Prussia. There is a fourteenth-century Father Time with a sickle and a twentieth-century Lord Burnham in a dinner jacket with his spectacles. Edmund Waller has been represented, with laurel leaves in his hair.

When Colin Mantripp started work, the lodge was covered with thick black bitumen. Sometimes the carvings were only half there; others were powdered wood in a shell of the tar; often there was nothing left at all. There is a magnificent twisted column of lime-wood, 'nice and crisp for feathers' with birds perching on the twisting vines, carved from Mantripp's imagination, and the bulging plums and pears hanging either side of the front window were built up from the flat slices of wood that he found under the bitumen. The two eagle friezes on the façade perfectly sum up the excellence of Mantripp's work on the building: the top row is 'original', made up from what could be salvaged from both friezes, and the bottom row is totally new, incorporating laurel wreaths to signify Edmund Waller and the ram from Lord Burnham's coat of arms.

A LA RONDE

Devon

A LA RONDE HAS THE KIND OF MAGICAL STRANGENESS THAT A CHILD MIGHT DREAM OF, WITH TINY shoulder-width staircases encrusted with shells and fossils, diamond-shaped windows, painted birds with real feathers flying on the walls and minute triangular rooms behind sliding panels. It was built in 1795 by two cultivated cousins, the Misses Jane and Mary Parminter, as a culmination of their ten-year-long Grand Tour of Europe and their return to England. It is a cosmopolitan 'Cottage Ornée', modelled on the sixth-century Byzantine basilica of San Vitale in Ravenna and riddled with domestic gaiety.

Surprises and delights are to be found around every corner; the hexagonal central hall with its shell en-crusted gallery soaring to the skies appears to be at least three times the height of its modest thirty-five feet. There are eight elegantly arched doorways, each framed in a roll of moulding of marbled dark green and each with a charmingly convenient secret bench to be let down for extra comfort when sitting out a dance. The eighteenth-century chairs which would appear to have been made for the hall provide equally sharp seating arrangements. With great wisdom, the Misses Parminter arranged their extraordinary house so that the central hall, with its scanty and rising heat, could be avoided throughout the winter months. Every room within its sixteen walls was interconnected and you could walk from one to the other, through magnifi-cently decorated chambers and three feet narrowing to six inches wide fully furnished 'wedges'. The house could be cosily enjoyed without putting your nose into the hall's chilly wastes.

Picturesque practicality was pursued throughout. A La Ronde was built so that daily life should progress with the sun: it rose into the bedrooms, shone into the

The shell gallery

Frieze of game birds' feathers in the drawing room

Detail of the drawing room

The eighteenth-century children's library

*A corner of the drawing room with
eighteenth-century scraps*

A thatched model of the house and eighteenth-century paintbox in the oval sitting room

The shell gallery and the 1810 Jubilee Crown

library, drawing room and ante-room during the morning and afternoon, and set through the windows of the oval sitting room, which was used specifically for the sight of it sinking into the River Exe.

Jane Parminter was born in Lisbon, which must account for some of the very un-English flair of the house. Certainly an extraordinary frieze of feathers was based on a Portuguese tile design produced at the time of the Moors' invasion. In regular pairs of circles, it marches round the top of the drawing room walls. Nearly all the feathers were from the gamebirds plucked at the kitchen table: there were tame parrots and peacocks, but their hues do not seem to be part of the design. According to Ursula Tudor-Perkins, the descendant of Jane Parminter, who lives in the house today, 'moths never go near them, their colour has not changed and they are angled so that the dust does not settle'.

Jane's father was a flamboyant figure who had houses in Lisbon, Devon and London. He owned coffee houses in Fleet Street, a glass factory in Lisbon and a fleet of ships which exported wine to as far afield as Brazil. Many aspects of A La Ronde's architectural ingenuity must have come from the family's knowledge of ship building, where with space being at such a premium the 'wedges' might assume acceptable proportions. John Parminter had a great triumph when he invented a new form of concrete for the rebuilding of Lisbon after the earthquake of 1755. The king of Portugal built him a glass factory in gratitude.

Any changes suffered by A La Ronde over the years have been at the rather clumsy hand of the Revd Oswald Reichel in the early 1880s, the only man ever to have owned the house. The roof was originally thatched and without windows, with little dovecotes hanging from

Drawing room

Oval sitting room

Octagon

Dining room

Pantry

Hall

The shell staircase to the gallery

A corner of the drawing room

the eaves, a Byzantine cupola with a weathervane on its peak, and the walls were plastered white and rampant with honeysuckle. He added the rather ungainly square windows, undoubtedly to the relief of the servants who had toiled for years, virtually in the dark, behind the elegant latticed diamonds. The Revd Reichel also installed a terrifying heating system with little elephant trunk radiators in every room. One alone remains for a moment's mockery, but he has the last laugh: two bombs fell on the roof during the war and, had it still been thatched, A La Ronde would be no more.

High above the hall is A La Ronde's crowning glory: a shell, feather, sand and china, lichen and bone-encrusted gallery, reached by a tiny gothic grotto staircase. The steps slope so that you are forced to bend forwards, your shoulders are scrunched together by the walls and up you squeeze, past a house of quills and a grotto of shells with the walls and ceilings embedded with glistening protruberances, their mirrors and fossils ablaze. The gallery is an explosion of rarity: razor shells zig-zag, limpets are laid as petals in flowers, feathers are laid as birds. Seals, porcelain, fossils and minerals, a fir cone, a teapot spout and a horse's neck bone are all there, arranged in dazzling meticulous patterns, with every architectural line decoratively pronounced.

It took the cousins eleven years to make and, when it was finished, they painted an immense crown over the doorway, celebrating their triumph and the 1810 Golden Jubilee of George III and Queen Charlotte a year later. In the spring of 1811 Jane Parminter built a church in the grounds of the house, with four almshouses for 'spinster ladies' and a school for six orphan girls, strangely incorporated into the building. She died that summer, having finished all that she had set out to do. It had taken two women only thirteen years to create all the glories of A La Ronde.

The Hollywood Hall and hacienda exterior of Stainsby

STAINSBY HALL

Derbyshire

STAINSBY HALL IS A HACIENDA HOLLY-WOOD HOUSE SET DOWN IN THE FIELDS OF DERBYSHIRE AND LIVED IN BY FOUR Sikh brothers, Dilraj, Kauldip, Lakhpal and Jagit Sandhu, who own a video shop, supermarkets and a fish bar in Tamworth, Kirk Hallam and Burton. They live in the building with their wives and six children, having found the house in 1987, and they are delighted with their buy. 'It is great and lovely, it is a rare structure, there is nothing like it in all England.'

It was built in 1973 on the site of the late eighteenth-century and mid-nineteenth-century Stainsby Hall, a nine-bay, grey stone and stucco pedimented building that had been demolished the year before. This had had four staircases, with a double sweep in the hall, and a wealth of stained glass. It was in a ruinous and rat-infested state, with shreds of curtains and pieces of dusty furniture in all the rooms when it was pulled down for its terrifying transmogrification.

The new Stainsby Hall was built by Nottingham architect David Shelley, for Robert Morley, a packaging millionaire. They wanted 'no square spaces, no box shapes', and they have succeeded in that there is barely a straight line in the house. The internal walls swerve and sweep off in all directions and, instead of doors, there are arches, either open or with bronzed, wrought iron gates with gilded points. The bathrooms are oval, with circular baths or showers; the main bedroom has a 'serpentine dressing area' and the kitchen has a forty-foot curving formica worktop. The front doors are made of panels of glass, coated with a bronze film that allows you to see out but not in. There is an immense and swirling open space in the hall and a curving cantilevered staircase with wrought iron bannisters and with the stairs themselves and the floor covered in the same mosaic as the showers and swimming pool. The pool, complete with a bar, is in a vast seventy-five foot long building all of its own, with waving walls, glass doors that slide open onto the terrace and great clerestory windows. The house is fully air conditioned, wired throughout for hi-fi; and there is a helicopter pad on the edge of the eighteen acre garden.

The Morleys had to sell their astonishing home after only eighteen months, when it was bought by a Mr Wong Henry (described as 'A Mystery Man from the Far East' in the *Ilkeston Advertiser and Erewash Valley Weekly News*) for only a third of the asking price: it had been on the market for £450,000 and went for £150,000. It was never lived in by Mr Wong Henry and after ten years was sold again; the verdict was that 'It was much more of a trouble having it than not having it.'

My friend David Rowbotham remembers going there in 1974: 'It was blinding white outside, with a great big silver Rolls Royce. It was very swirly inside,

with no straight lines at all and my whole impression was of apricot; everything was in peach and apricot.'

After a colourful life of only fifteen years, Stainsby Hall is now in even more exotic and very happy hands.

The exterior of Stainsby

SIR THOMAS TRESHAM BUILT THE TRIANGULAR LODGE AT RUSHTON BETWEEN JULY 28 1594 AND SEPTEMBER 29 1597. It is a pious and exquisite Elizabethan conceit, designed both to symbolise the Holy Trinity and as an elaborate pun on Tresham's name and his emblem of a trefoil.

Everything about the little building revolves around the number three. Each side of the triangle is thirty-three feet four inches long, one third of a hundred, which tapers up to thirty-three feet, and there are three storeys, with three windows on each side. The three main rooms are hexagonal, each with a triangular corner chamber. Nine gables soar up to the sky, ablaze with stone flames, creatures and three-sided pinnacles topped with trefoils.

Each side of the building represents one member of the Holy Trinity, with unifying inscriptions which are carried round all three façades. Eighteen letters, MENTES TUORUM VISITA (Visit the minds of Thy people), are incised above the windows and RESPICITE NON MIHI SOLI LABORAVI (Behold not for myself alone have I laboured) is written above the sundials in the central gables. Carved on either side, on the south-east face, are the emblems of the seven-branched candlestick and the seven eyes of God, to represent God the Father. To the north, the hen with her chicks and 'the pelican in her piety' represent God the Son; and to the south-west, the dove on a serpent and the hand of God represent the Holy Ghost. The entablature, thirty-three feet long on each side, has three passages from the Bible, each with thirty-three letters: APERIATUR TERRA ET GERMINET SALVATOREM (Let the earth open and bring forth a saviour) on the south-east face; QUIS SEPARABIT NOS A CHARITATE CHRISTI (Who will separate us from the love of Christ) to the north, and CONSIDERAVI OPERA TUA DOMINE ET EXPAVI (I have considered thy works O Lord

and been afraid) to the south-west.

Nine stone angels with lead pipes sticking out of their stomachs and with letters incised on their chests project from beneath the frieze. Those on the angles have a triangle in a circle incised on the soffit, the other six have letters: SS SD DS and QEE QEE QVE, the initials of SANCTUS SANCTUS SANCTUS DOMINUS DEUS SABAOTH . . . QUI ERAT ET QUI EST ET QUI VENTURUS EST (Holy Holy Holy Lord God of Sabaoth which was and is and is to come).

The chimney, topped with the trefoils of Tresham and the Trinity, soars into the sky, carved with emlems on each of its three sides – the sacred monogram IHS with the cross and the three nails, the Lamb of God in a square, to symbolise the four evangelists, and a Tau cross in a chalice enclosed in a pentagon to symbolise salvation.

Tresham family shields surround the windows, with a dazzling variation of trefoils on the top floor and crosses with trefoils at the end of each arm on the ground. Little trefoils with a triangular opening light the basement. The words TRES TESTIMONIUM DANT (There are three that bear witness) are incised over the front door.

Thomas Tresham spent fifteen years either in prison or in confinement for his religious beliefs. It is said that he was brought up as a Protestant – he was knighted by Queen Elizabeth in 1575 – but he was certainly a Catholic by 1581 when he was sent to prison for sheltering Campion, with hefty recusancy fines of nearly £6,000.

This building is a sermon in stone, a proclamation of his faith.

*Marble reclining
figure in the hall*

BRODSWORTH HALL
Yorkshire

THE EXTERIOR OF BRODSWORTH HALL IS SOLIDLY AND STRAIGHTFORWARDLY NEO-CLASSICAL; INSIDE IT IS A FOREST of columns and statues marching about the great halls and corridors of the house. With marbled, gilded, damask and mirrored walls and the thousandfold reflections of naked marble mothers cuddling naked marble babies, the effect is of an astonishing and unlimited opulence.

It was built between 1861 and 1870 by Phillip Wilkinson to the designs of Chevalier Casentini, an Italian architect from Lucca, who, it is thought, never put his foot in England, let alone on Yorkshire soil. It is not known how much was built to his schemes but, architecturally, the atmosphere is steeped in Southern climes with the columned 'courtyards' of the halls, the parade of marble statuary and the 'cloisters' of the arcaded and mirrored corridor. Space flows into space, with Minton tiles and matching Axminster carpets underfoot, stretching off in every direction.

No modernising hand (not even the plumber's, there are several handsome valve closets) has been laid on the house since it was finished in 1870. The library and the study are still hung with their handblocked and brilliantly gilded wallpapers and the original damask still glows on the furniture, curtains and walls. It hangs in the drawing room and it is draped into ornate pelmets over the alarming nineteenth-century shuttering system. On either side of every downstairs window hang thick ropes with leaden weights; one haul, a terrifying crash, and an impenetrable curtain of slats falls to the ground outside.

Brodsworth was built with the proceeds of a curious and celebrated will made in 1797 by a Swiss banker called Peter Thellusson. He left £700,000, stipulating that it was to accumulate at compound interest during the lifetimes of his sons and his sons' sons. Over the years thousands of pounds were spent by the enraged family, contesting the will, and, by 1859 when the House of Lords pronounced in favour of two great-grandsons, Charles Sabine Thellusson and Lord Rendlesham, there was little left of the original capital. A coal mine and the Brodsworth estate was Thellusson's share and, after demolishing the Georgian house, he set to work building a palace.

'It was built to impress,' said the late Silvia Grant-Dalton, who lived at Brodsworth for nearly sixty years, 'with its size, the length of its drive, how many pine-apples there were on the roof or something like that; it was such a dotty way to judge people; I do think that they were really rather horrid sometimes.' She married Charles Grant-Dalton (Thellusson's nephew) when she was only sixteen. He had made up his mind to marry her when she was twelve and he was thirty. 'He was always in the nursery, making such a botheration of himself, which made Nanny and then my governess in a rage. "Why can't he have tea in the drawing room like everybody else?"' He died in 1944 and eight years later Silvia married his first cousin, Eustace Grant-Dalton. 'Dear old Eustace, he was such a brave man, he got into all the wars he could; Queen Victoria signed his first commission for the Boer War and he fought in the Kaiser's War and the last war. When he died he left me the house to look after and I haven't left it for a single day.' She grew fond of Brodsworth, although she has always much preferred Georgian architecture. 'I don't care for the sentimentality of Victorian times . . . the statues, which I call the 'poor cold ladies' to the chil-dren, are not quite my gusto, I'm afraid.'

The house is now in grave peril; should Silvia's daughter not want to live there, this electrifying time warp of nineteenth-century country life will go for ever.

Limitless views through the summer hall and corridor

CLAYDON HOUSE

Buckinghamshire

THE CHINESE ROOM AT CLAYDON HOUSE WAS CARVED BY LUKE LIGHTFOOT, 'AN IGNORANT KNAVE WITH NO small spice of madness in his composition.' These were the despairing words of Sir Thomas Robinson, written to Lord Verney in 1769, trying to convince him of Lightfoot's dishonesty.

Ralph, second Earl Verney had inherited the Tudor manor house of Claydon in 1752 and, with the fashionable tastes of an immensely rich Whig, landowner and peer, had drawn up plans for a house in the classical style, employing Lightfoot as the architect, master mason, carver and surveyor of works. Plasterwork and carving of unrivalled glory were the outcome, with classical, rococo and gothic motifs swarming all over the walls, culminating in the Chinese Room, one of the most extraordinary sights in England. But it was all at a terrible cost to Lord Verney, who had been tricked and deceived at every turn for over ten years.

He had first met Lightfoot in 1757, when he considered him to be 'a very honest, able and skilful Architect'. Earl Verney was a much better judge of the proportions of a cornice than of the honesty of a middleman according to Margaret Maria Lady Verney, writing of him in 1930. All the work was to be under Lightfoot's direction but he seldom went to Claydon and the workmen stood idle. All the materials, the wood, stone and marble, (one fireplace from Italy, covered with writhing babies, cost £1,000) were to be under his control but, as well as secretly selling what he could to line his own pockets, he often claimed that he had bought more than he had. '. . . the more you sift into this ignorant Villain's conduct . . . the more you will be astonished,' wrote Sir Thomas Robinson in another letter, suggesting that the 'Rogue' be brought to Justice. As a 'last dernier resort' to avoid litigation,

Taking tea in the alcove in the Chinese Room

Sir Thomas was dispatched to see Lightfoot: 'He received me in his parlour with his Hat on his head, an austere look, fierce as an Eastern Monarch, his Eyes sparkl'd fire, his countenance angry and revengeful – did not ask me to sit down . . .'

The mission failed; the Chancery case of Verney v. Lightfoot was heard on 12 April 1771 with the claim that of the £30,000 paid to Lightfoot for work and materials, only £7,000 could be accounted for. A compromise was reached with Lightfoot making over properties to Verney. He retired to Dulwich in 1779 to become a victualler. A footnote to the whole affair is that his son, Theophilus Lightfoot, emigrated to Australia, where the family name survives, using 'Verney' as a Christian name in each succeeding generation.

Sir Thomas Robinson was commissioned by Lord Verney to embellish Claydon still further in 1769, when a palace of colossal proportions was planned to outshine all his neighbours, one of which, as ill luck would have it for his pride and his pocket, was Stowe with what Horace Walpole called its 'inexpressible richness'. Both men were 'unfettered by considerations of prudence'. Robinson, described as looking like a pair of scissors, 'a giant whose legs would scarcely support him', was a 'gentleman architect' who lived, as well as built, on a magnificent scale. Verney's tastes can be relished in the Chinese Room and in a description of his equipage: 'a brace of tall negroes, with silver French horns, behind his coach and six, perpetually making a noise, like Sir Henry Sidney's Trompeters in the days of Elizabeth, bloweing very joyfully to behold and see.'

Their building was just as ostentatious, and it was to be their downfall: Lord Verney was ruined by the expenditure and died a bankrupt in 1791. A year later it was all demolished, with Lightfoot's wing left to stand alone.

THE PINEAPPLE HOUSE

Stirlingshire

THE PINEAPPLE HOUSE AT DUNMORE WAS BUILT FOR THE TWENTY-NINE-YEAR-OLD FOURTH EARL OF DUNMORE in 1761. A huge and perfectly proportioned stone fruit, it bursts out of an elegant octagon, with seven ogival-headed windows and a slender front door. The back of the house looms above the once splendid vegetable garden, reached by curving stairways. The entrance front sits elegantly on the ground.

There were six acres of walled garden at Dunmore in the eighteenth and nineteenth centuries, producing a succulent harvest of pineapples, peaches and other rare fruits, and the wonderful little building may well have been a symbol of these horticultural triumphs. The architect is not known but it is thought that William Gilpin laid out the gardens and grounds on the site of a quarry.

The arrangements at Dunmore were picturesquely elaborate: as well as the pineapple looming overall, the stone furnace chimneys on the main north wall were disguised as classical urns. A number of stoves were built into the wall, which was over three foot thick and riddled with channels and flues to trap the warm air. Hot houses flanked a Tuscan columned portico, that still stands directly under the pineapple and through which you pass to climb one of two flights of steps round and up to the front of the building. On either side of the house, at ground floor level, there are little stone bothies where the gardeners would have lived.

Curiously, there is no mention of a house at Dunmore until 1820, when William Wilkins built a rather dull castellated pile (demolished in 1972), and it would appear that this little luscious pineapple kingdom stood by itself, south-east of Stirling. The Dunmores lived at Glen Finart in Argyleshire, nearly 300 miles away, to where the exotic fruits were regularly dispatched. In

1812 Lord Dunmore's grandson, Sir Charles Murray, wrote of their startling novelty with the Highlanders. The Laird of Auchnashalloch had paid a call. 'His manners were very primitively rough, and his stock of English was very scant . . . Lunch having been announced, of course he was invited to go into the dining-room, and he looked, with some surprise, at the display of fruit on the table. We had no hothouse fruit at the glen, but a supply was sent every fortnight from Dunmore Park, where my father had no house, but an excellent garden. After he had dispatched the solids, he pointed to a dish on which were three or four very fine peaches, and he said, "What kind of an apple is yon?" So my mother told him that we called it a peach, and he said, "Well, I'll just tak yen to taste." He accordingly took a peach and stuck half of it into his mouth, and bit hard into it. The juice ran out of the sides of his mouth, and he said, "Oh, it's a gran' apple; but siccan a pip as it's got!"'

A surprising association with the refined elegance of the Pineapple House is that it was built for a man who was to become known as the 'Bloody Butcher' of the American War of Independence. When the Earl of Dunmore was Governor of New York and of Virginia, he was renowned for his ruthlessness, destroying Indian villages and forcing the tribes to abandon all claims to their lands. In 1775 he commandeered the gunpowder from the Williamsburg arsenal and, taking command of two men-of-war and a flotilla of British ships, he ransacked and ravaged the Virginian coastline for over a year and was responsible for reducing the town of Norfolk to ashes.

The Pineapple House was given to the National Trust of Scotland and is now on long lease to the Landmark Trust who have restored it, with the help of the Historic Buildings Council and the Tourist Board.

MONKTON HOUSE

Sussex

ONKTON HOUSE WAS SOLD, ALONG WITH SOME OF ITS CONTENTS, IN 1986. CONTROVERSY HAD RAGED as to whether or not it was worth preserving. It was seen as both a perfect dream and a hideous nightmare of Surrealism but, as the lone representative in England of this bizarre movement, it should have been saved, either for our delight or for our derision.

It was built and elaborately clad in brick by Sir Edwin Lutyens for Mr and Mrs Willie James in 1902 as a retreat from the grandeur of West Dean, their house some five miles away (now the excellent Edward James Foundation), and transformed into this startling surrealistic conceit by their son Edward James thirty years later.

He himself was a surprising figure. When alone at Monkton, he would stride naked about the woods, with Radio Three blaring out from loud speakers on the roof. As often as not, the music would change into roaring philosophical talk. He had led a lively life; one of his earliest memories was of seeing the butler present Edward VII with a giant box tied up with a pink ribbon, in which his mother was lying dressed up as a doll with wax on her face and a key attached to her chest, labelled 'Wind here'. When this was done, Mrs James had danced 'mechanically' round the room. 'That sort of thing kept him [the King] amused.'

The James family was immensely rich and Edward spent lavishly throughout his life, either as a serious patron of the arts, most particularly of the Surrealists – he was the first to support Dali – or on the development of his own fanciful ideas. Always he had violent tastes: as an undergraduate in Oxford he painted his ceiling purple, with a two-foot-deep quotation from Seneca, in gold, along a mauve frieze. Dali advised him on the work at Monkton and, with architect Christopher Nicolson, assisted by Hugh Casson, and with Norris

Purple paint, concrete linen, iron palm trees and bamboo drainpipes

The spare bedroom

The bathroom

Wakefield in charge of the decoration, the house was brilliantly transformed.

The walls are painted purple over peacock blue and the front door is sugar pink. Plaster 'linen' hangs out of the windows, in imitation of sheets being aired; plaster folds loop round the bathroom window and drape over the clock on the roof, which shows the days of the week rather than the hours. The drainpipes are fashioned to look like bamboo and life-size iron palm trees stand on either side of the entrance. The roof had to be heightened to accommodate these essential embellishments.

Inside, Lutyens has vanished without trace: the staircase sweeps up in an Odeon cinema curve, past a fish tank inset into the wall which, as well as being full of fish, once gave an oblique view of the guest bathroom and of the guest in the bath. The wallpaper was printed as the exact match (including the stitching) of the Italian material that lines the walls of the corridors of the house. The carpet, woven with the footprints of James's Irish wolfhound, must have been a miserable symbol of his failed marriage to the dancer Tilly Losch, whose footprints had been woven into the stair-carpet at West Dean.

The drawing room was originally to be decorated like the lining of a dog's stomach, with flapping and 'breathing' walls. 'Mae West's lips' were the sofas in the dining room, and stars shone on the illuminated glass ceiling of the spare bedroom. Edward James's bed, inspired by Nelson's hearse, stood in a room entirely covered with shimmering chicken wire.

Most glorious of all was the circular bathroom with its dome of Styrian jade and walls of pink alabaster through which shone a golden sun and a silver moon.

ST. CRISPIN'S TEMPLE

Buckinghamshire

St. Crispin's Temple, apparently an enchanting flint and brick church, is in fact a cottage. It stands on the edge of the West Wycombe estate and is one of the many elegant curiosities built by the notorious Sir Francis Dashwood, Chancellor of the Exchequer to George III, founder of the satanic Hell-fire Club, profligate and lecher, a man who, according to Wraxall, 'far exceeded in licentiousness anything exhibited since Charles the Second'.

Sir Francis was an alarming figure, deranged yet distinguished. As a Fellow of the Royal Society, founder member of the Dilettanti Society and Lord Lieutenant of Buckinghamshire, he was known to have disguised himself as Charles XII of Sweden and, travelling into Russia, paid serious court to the Czarinà Anne in St. Petersburg. On another Grand Tour in the 1720s he enacted the Devil in Rome, an incident which Walpole describes as having 'made a great noise at the time'.

The Devil was regularly invoked in Buckingham-shire, beneath the obscenely frescoed ceilings of Medmenham Abbey, the ancient ruin leased by Sir Francis in 1752 and richly embellished for his unedifying companions, the 'Knights of St. Francis of Wycombe' of the Hell-fire Club. Lord Sandwich was one, the First Lord of the Admiralty, 'as mischievous as a monkey and as lecherous as a goat', a man who was described by Lord Chesterfield as following 'an unblushing course of debauchery and dissipation'. There were politicians and poets, doctors, pamphleteers, artists and peers who all roistered together with the 'slaves of their lust', women dressed as nuns, in the thick incense-laden air of the evil Masses. Black tapers were lit around an inverted crucifix and burning herbs with bitumen, henbane, vervain and serin thickened the atmosphere with smoke. Wine was drunk from skulls and, surrounded by lascivious

statuary and 'horrifying' works of art, the 'friars' in white linen robes plunged on with their debaucheries.

Bubb Doddington, the 'Puffy Peer' Lord Melcombe, was another brother. He was a man of immense size, rich and vain, whose marbled and gilded house in Hammersmith, hung with imitation icicles, was named 'La Trappe', again in mockery of monastic life. When the 'Knights' gathered, he would thunder his corpulent way down to Buckinghamshire in a golden coach drawn by six black horses, and when he died he left £500 to Sir Francis, to commemorate his glory with an arch, temple, column or additional room. They are all there, in the one curious hexagon open to the skies – one hundred and fifty yards in circumference, it looms heavily on Wycombe Hill, overlooking the estate that is crammed with Sir Francis Dashwood's architectural conceits. There are temples, arches and bridges, an aggrandised farm house with little gazebos overlooking a lake and a round lodge, two classical lodges, a sham lodge, the temple of Daphne, a pyramid roof on Doric columns. Caves were excavated into the hills with a gothic arched entrance; the Church of St. Lawrence was classicised and the house rebuilt in Italian splendour with frescoed walls and ceilings inside and out.

The park is an 'oasis of the picturesque', with little eighteenth-century buildings at every turn in its land-scape. High Wycombe, wrecked by the influence of 'Silicon Valley' nearby, has been built up to its walls and the shock of stepping from one to the other is extraor-dinary. St. Crispin's is on its very edge, facing the industry and backing onto the parkland.

St. Crispin was the patron saint of shoemakers and St. Crispin's Day is Monday, the day of rest for cob-blers. Perhaps this chapel-like exterior mockingly shel-tered an extra day of rollicking for the Knights of St. Francis of Wycombe.

Imperatrix cum Apro

CARDIFF CASTLE

Wales

ARDIFF CASTLE IS THE GLORIOUS TRIUMPH OF THE THIRD MARQUIS OF BUTE AND HIS ARCHITECT AND FRIEND, William Burges. It is a little town of towers, each one filled with a jumble of jewel-like rooms, all ablaze with architectural and decorative riches.

Lord Bute was only eighteen years old when he first met Burges and, when he came of age in 1868, they embarked upon their brilliantly eclectic architectural schemes together. They were both raging romantics, obsessed with medievalism and craftsmanship and their dreams exploded into an extraordinary reality at Cardiff Castle. Every room is encrusted with rich and intricate decoration, designed with serious scholarship and riddled through with veins of humour that make you laugh out loud at their fun. The Clock Tower was begun in 1869 and it was built throughout on the theme of time with, outside, figures representing the planets flanking the four gilded faces of the clock and, inside, a wealth of symbolic detail. After a one-hundred-and-one-step toil to the top, the Summer Smoking Room bursts upon you. It is gay, lively, colourful and light, shone over by a gilded Apollo on the chandelier with the rays of the sun beneath him. This gleaming room represents the universe, with a map of the world in silver, copper and bronze in the centre of the floor, surrounded by tiles of man, mammals, birds and fish. The God of Love, with a lovebird on each wrist, sits on the hood of the fireplace, above a frieze of romantic summer pastimes. The eight winds of Greek mythology act as corbels over the great tiled frieze of the legends of the zodiac.

The Winter Smoking Room is at the bottom of the tower; you pass under the grotesque ebony face of Typhon (representing chaos), his ivory fangs at the ready, and over the hounds of Hell inset in mosaic into the floor. When you shut the door, it becomes part of the shimmering walnut panelling inlaid with mother of pearl and box, with its grotesque and mythological creatures, prancing all round the room. The door itself is inlaid with entrancing musical animals: a mouse beating a drum and a parrot reading a score. Burges particularly loved the parrot with 'its grotesque motions, its fine colouring and its great intelligence'. The door handle is another, and they perch and fly all over the castle's walls, floors and ceilings. The massive fireplace in the Winter Smoking Room is made from one block of Forest of Dean stone which was brought to Cardiff and carved on the spot. Under the inscription 'Love conquers all let us yield to love', the pleasures of winter are paraded above the fire: great hounds lie at a hearth, a figure loads his cross bow, another practises archery and a lady bedecked in mauve, pink and gold is skating on shinbone blades. Four giant corbels representing Sunrise, Day, Sunset and Night look down on the room from each corner.

The castle was a cauldron of inventive talent, the Bute Workshops had been set up in Cardiff and Burges had a tried and trusted team of men, whose names should all be cheered to the skies: Horatio Walter Lonsdale, Fred Weekes, Charles Campell, Nathaniel Westlake and Frederick Smallfield were the decorative artists, Thomas Nicolls, Ceccardo Fucigna and William Clarke were the sculptors. The wood carving and marquetry, in at least a dozen different woods such as avodire and French Charbonnier walnut, was wrought by Thomas John and his sons Thomas and William. The tiles were produced by W. B. Simpson and Sons, William Godwin and George Maw. Three architects worked under Burges: William Frame, John Starling Chapple and his brother-in-law, Ricard Popplewell Pullan.

The Arab Room in the Herbert Tower, with its

Monkey bell push in the small dining room

Mice in the small dining room

A creature creeps over the castle wall

The Arab Room ceiling

Animal decorations in the Winter Smoking Room

The Winter Smoking Room fireplace

Corbels representing sunrise,

day

and sunset

74

scarlet and gold leafed Islamic ceiling, is their most exotic creation. The walls and floor are entirely of marble, with gilded parrots and niches, and wall cabinets mounted in silver. It was built in the year of Burges's death and inscribed in alabaster over the fireplace are the words, 'John Marquis of Bute built this in 1881, William Burges designed it.'

The fireplaces throughout are architectural gems in their own right. In the Banqueting Hall, the overmantel sprouts a castle with figures blowing trumpets on the battlements, a portcullis and a gloomy prisoner peering from a cell. Robert, Earl of Gloucester, rides off, being waved to from above by his wife Matilda, while Robert 'Curthose' (short legged) Duke of Normandy gazes at them from behind bars. Creatures from *The Mabinogion*, a collection of Welsh folk tales, embellish the walls, a giant frog, a boar, and one of the most beguiling of all the details in Cardiff Castle, a salmon that swims through the wall.

The Chaucer Room has the quality of fairyland, with every inch most delicately decorated, soaring upwards into the lantern of the octagonal tower. Chaucer presides overall, surrounded by the birds of his 'Parliament of Foules', and above a series of paintings and sculptures of the 'Legend of Good Women'. The thirty-two stained glass windows illustrate *The Canterbury Tales*.

The small dining room has a richly splendid ceiling and fireplace with little oaks growing up through the hood, their roots splaying out below. The Greek inscription, 'Entertaining Angels Unawares', is carved amidst grotesque faces, some with their tongues sticking out, and three angels tell Sarah and Abraham that they are expecting a child. Sarah, aged ninety-two, sits laughing with her hand over her mouth.

Any glance, in any direction, at Cardiff Castle gives surprise, delight and pleasure.

EAGLE ROCK

Sussex

WITH ITS 'BODY AND WINGS' TO LIVE IN, ITS 'HEAD' FOR A LOFT, AND ITS 'BEAK' TO SHELTER cars, Eagle Rock is like a huge glass and steel bird. It was built between 1982 and 1983 by Ian Ritchie for a retired lady botanist. The house is sheltered on three sides by crags of sandstone rock, with an eagle-shaped formation looming up over the 'tail' from the north. The site, found quite by chance through *Exchange and Mart*, complete with a bungalow that had to be blown up, determined the design of the building.

Both architect and client wanted the house to link with the garden and the garden to link with the wild. Ritchie's initial scheme would have appeared as almost indigenous to the plot. He planned a completely transparent canopy, reinforced with stainless steel wire, which was to stretch from rock to rock and under which there would be wooden rooms. This would enable you to wander through the trees, but protected from snow, wind and rain. 'Under it we would have been able to design very precise timber enclosures . . . you would not have had to face the problems of waterproofing, so you could have made them as precise and beautiful as pieces of furniture.' However, this plan entailed coring and concrete filling the sandstone, which the client did not approve of, and so the 'bird' was born.

In the end, fifteen tons of rock had to be removed to settle the house into its 'bowl', and also because Ritchie felt strongly that the 'natural sunlit room' on the southern side, where the lawn and garden flourish, should not be encroached upon. The inside merges happily with the outside: the floors are exactly the same colour as the paving; the would-be barriers of the walls are either of glass (which slide away) or sand-coloured cladding (now covered with mesh panels entwined with creepers) which blur into the surrounding greenery. Both the

client and Ritchie now regret that there is not still more glass, giving more vistas into and through the house from all directions. 'Views should not cease on entry,' says Ritchie. The 'tail feathers' of the conservatory can be seen through the framing of the front door, the spare bedroom on the tip of the east 'wing' appears to be gouged out of the rock with only glass separating it from the sandstone. Two vistas in the house end with triangular windows, reflecting the shape of the steel structure: 'Oriental paintings,' Ritchie calls them, 'a little picture frame of the landscape outside that changes with the seasons.'

The original idea of a floating canopy was not totally abandoned. One of the most exciting details of Eagle Rock is that the 'wings' are actually suspended from the central spine of the house, making you feel that it could suddenly heave into life and flap away. Their roofs are elaborately insulated, passively conserving solar energy using double glazing, solar collector panels, air ducts, glass fibre insulation, vapour barriers, insulated louvre blinds et cetera, as well as solar control blinds to imitate bird feathers. The 'head' is the energy centre of the house, with the water and central heating systems.

The steel frame arrived in a kit from London. Ritchie wanted it to be black with red joints, like 'a piece of sculpture in a natural environment, not a camouflaged piece of sculpture . . . and highlighting the component parts in red would have really made it sing'. The client, with her passion for plants, was keen to camouflage, to have a layer of greenery between the building and the landscape. What has emerged is a spirited compromise that must excite wonder in both the scoffer and the sympathiser.

HULL MASTER BUILDER, DAVID REYNARD ROBINSON, WAS A MAN OF REMARKABLY ADVANCED TASTES who left his idiosyncratic mark on local schools, churches, public houses, convents and warehouses. But nowhere was it laid more violently than on 'Farrago', the curious ceramic home which he built between 1908 and 1909, for his retirement, when he was seventy-two years old.

Tiles had always blazed out of his buildings: his office in Hull, dating from 1876, had been entirely covered with them, and the circular floor, ceiling and walls were decorated in brilliantly bold abstract designs of orange, black, brown, blue, yellow, pink and white. It was modern art and it was Gaudi, all in an extraordinary jumble. His office, in Freehold Street, Hull, has been demolished, but every tile was saved by Josie Montgomery, the Curator of the Scarborough Art Gallery, who now lives in 'Farrago' and is devoting her life to restoring and repairing everything of David Reynard Robinson's that she can lay her hands on. Her eyes gleam when she describes his work. 'His office was an astonishing piece of modern art. It is what the abstract American Expressionists were doing in the 40s and 50s with its totally abstract composition of movement, shapes, colour and rhythms deliberately put together . . . a glorious mash of colour to look at.'

'Farrago' is a glorious mash of colour from top to toe, its walls and floors all shining away around you. Robinson made deliberate and grotesque mistakes with every pattern, so enticing you to seek them all out, following every zig zag, curve and twist as you go. Architecturally the doorcases are often jammed into the tiles where they should not be, with all symmetry abandoned, and this too gives you a jolt and makes you stop and study it again with care. It is like being in a huge slippery

The exterior

The larder floor

The tiled tunnel of the staircase

The larder

smooth maze of colour. Josie is sure that 'he was trying to jump into the twentieth century when he built the house . . . it's cocking a snook at Victorian decoration, at a normal way of building, but it's also breaking away from traditional patterns and this is a sort of way of jumping into modern art, it's an early way of thinking about what was developing over the turn of the century.'

The floors of the back yard and outside lavatory (reached by some tortuously steep and narrow steps and now enclosed to make the kitchen) are the most futuristic surfaces in the house, with fragments of broken tiles coursed through with brilliant blue ceramic circles. To have designed this in 1908 is strange enough, but to have designed it to pave the back yard of a house in Yorkshire in 1908 is a startling triumph!

His eye-catching 'mistakes' are curious, unexpected and often difficult to find. Usually one tile is totally at odds with the meticulous pattern surrounding it, or they might alter their colour or number in a sequence. Robinson used Dutch and Spanish tiles, both hand-painted and transfer-printed, as well as William Morris's little blue and yellow daisy design in the dining room. There is one William de Morgan tile in the ceramic-lined wash-house and grandest of all is the flawless arrangement of Maw's encaustic tiles on the landing. The staircase is like a bejewelled tunnel, with a riot of colour bearing down on you from all sides.

Outside the tiles rampage on. David Reynard Robinson's son-in-law, who had built the substantial red house next door, was so embarrassed by the sight of 'Farrago' that he put up a twenty-foot high wall between them. When Josie bought the house, the entire façade had been painted white and only now, some ten years later, has she managed to reveal most of the ceramic embellishments – a castle is still hidden under

The landing with encaustic tiles

the gable – although many will have to be renewed. She has saved many tiles from Robinson's demolished buildings and plans to return them to their former glory. She has saved whole panels as well, including everything from a bathroom which was covered from wall to ceiling with bright blue, orange, pink, green, black and white tiles, in every imaginable combination.

The gazebo is lined throughout with floral patterns and its floor is embedded with fragments. The flowerbeds are surrounded with great pieces of tiles set into strips of cement and huge decorative chimney pots, again rescued by Josie, are standing by, ready to be hoisted aloft to crown David Reynard Robinson's masterpiece. Some are original to 'Farrago', the others were saved from his demolished houses.

The house has recently been listed, as much because of its steel frame structure, decoratively clad, as for its astonishing tilework, and, of course, because of Josie's

stirling efforts. She is frustrated by the fact that all Robinson's records were destroyed by his daughter but she tirelessly battles on, winkling out local information and saving what she can. The spirit and verve of David Reynard Robinson lives on (his ghost has made itself heard in the rooms for years) with Josie Montgomery's exhaustive and imaginative plans for the house's restoration.

The dining room

Highfort Court

Bartizans for the dustbins

KINGSBURY

London

AN ARCHITECTURAL TOUR ROUND THE STREETS OF KINGSBURY IN NORTH LONDON GIVES YOU A LOT of shocks: small castles rear up on some corners and timber-framed and thatched country cottages stand on others. There are houses clad entirely in weaving wood or decorated with bricks laid in elaborate patterns; some have outsize, twisted chimneys with entrance arches in their stacks, and there are gables and bays of every description. It is all the work, much of it pioneering, of Ernest Trobridge, done between 1921 and 1937.

Trobridge was an architect who was convinced that the post-war housing crisis could be overcome by using traditional building methods on a mass scale, producing low cost but interesting and individual houses. He particularly recommended elm, 'not as an antiquarian enthusiast but as a practical architect'. As well as being cheap, 'one shilling a square foot', it was in plentiful supply and had been rejected by builders because it warped and twisted as it dried. This he used to his advantage and it waves and curves all over his houses, both inside and out.

He recommended thatch as well, weighing a third and costing a quarter of a tiled roof. He patented his plans and, by 1920, was selling estates as well as whole villages, estates on which no two houses were the same. Most surprising of all on the estate at Kingsbury are two blocks of flats disguised as forts.

Whitecastle Mansion encloses five flats, two reached by the staircase, two through the 'moat' and one from behind. Beneath the great tower of a chimney at High-fort Court, a Gaudian medieval entrance sweeps you up over another 'moat' of a basement to the front doors beneath the arch. The rooms inside, all on different levels, were originally lined with oak plywood panell-ing and fitted radiant bars. The flat roof was built especially for sunbathing with a deckchair store in the ramparts and, either side of the stairs, there are two little bartizans with arrow loop openings for the dustbins!

Trobridge was an ardent follower of Swedenborgian philosophy, which 'affects every detail of every structure, enabling one to divide each problem into end, cause and effect . . . I am convinced that this philosophy will soon completely change construction.' His last and oddest building was the Hotel Ozonia on Canvey Island in Essex. It was enormous, with bulging bays clad in twisted elm and a tiny thatched roof. The inside walls were painted with murals of an aquarium, of koala bears and of a stone cell with creatures peering through the cracks. It was built as a modestly priced hotel for holiday makers from the East End and, in that role, was one of the few buildings which realised Trobridge's ambition of building for the masses. His previous patrons had, for the most part, been private.

Whitecastle Mansion

It is sad that his dreams were not fulfilled, a utopia of council estates made up of castles and timber-framed cottages cladding the land.

THE HUER'S HOUSE
Cornwall

THE LITTLE HUER'S HOUSE, DATING FROM 1835, ONCE PLAYED A KEY ROLE IN NEWQUAY'S PILCHARD FISHING industry. It was from here that the Huer kept a look-out for the shoals of fish and, when they were sighted, either by a tinge of red in the sea or by flocks of gulls, he would roar out the good news with cries of 'heva heva!' and would blow through a megaphone longer than a coach horn. 'The cry is up, the cry is up!' would whip the town into a pitch of excitement and within minutes the boats were out. The Huer would then direct the fishermen from the flat roof of his house, waving his arms and a flag to guide them to the shadow on the water.

The method of fishing in Newquay was known as seining and every seining company workforce was organised in precise and picturesque terms. There were thirteen seines and each one had a cellar, a courtyarded and cloistered building where all the landwork was done. The Spy was the oldest, the Hope was the last to be built in 1871. They all had to be big enough to allow as many as 150,000 pilchards to be worked on within their walls. Each seine was allocated certain waters (stems or berths) in Newquay Bay and in the Gazzle which they had to change every twenty-four hours, from midnight to midnight, on a rotary system.

When 'the cry' went up, three boats pushed out to sea: the seine-boat with its thousand-foot long stop seine net, followed by the volyer with the tuck seine net and, last of all, the lurker with the master seiner who supervised and helped with the whole operation. The seine net made the initial catch and, if the water was too deep, it would be hauled to shallow waters, moored by little anchors and left until the next tide to settle the fish down. The pilchards were carried to the cellars in long wooden boxes called gurries or round baskets known as

mauns, and the bulking or salting work, that was always done by women and children, would begin. The pilchards were laid in overlapping rows in the cloisters, their tails to the wall and, as children sprinkled them with salt, they were stacked, one on top of the other, until there was a great wall of fish five foot high by two foot deep, their noses to the fore. Often it would get even bigger, so that the walls of the entire courtyard appeared to be built of pilchards' noses.

After six weeks, when the oil had drained away into a large pit, the fish walls were dismantled. The men prised them carefully apart with a wooden, spade-like instrument and placed the pilchards in a circular sieve called a wriggle, which was shaken by the women to loosen any remaining salt onto a wooden table or horse. The fish were borne off in gurries to be scrubbed clean with stiff brooms and, after a second washing, were packed, with the aid of stone weights, into square-sided barrels called hogsheads. Again the noses faced outwards, except for the middle of each layer which formed a 'rose' of alternating heads and tails. This was revealed when the barrel was dismantled for the buyers and a glistening block of some 3,000 pilchards, crowned with an elegant 'rose', stood waiting for inspection. The end of the season was celebrated with the troil, a feast in each cellar, with fiddling, singing, dancing and games.

Pilchard fishing was an important part of the Cornish economy for hundreds of years. In the 1590s an act of Parliament protected its interests and another in the early 1600s allowed Huers to rush onto anybody's property to yell their warnings without being had up for trespassing. But the seining industry had been in constant rivalry with the drifting method, and it finally died away in the 1890s when the pilchard changed its route and no longer swam near to the Cornish shores.

The Oak Room

SCARISBRICK

Lancashire

SCARISBRICK'S GREAT TOWER CAN BE SEEN FOR MILES AROUND, STANDING ALONE ON THE FLATNESS OF MARTIN MERE, near Southport in Lancashire. It was built in the 1860s by Edward Welby Pugin as a daringly out-of-scale addition to the house that had been designed by his father, Augustus Welby Pugin, between 1837 and 1845.

The elder Pugin's client was Charles Scarisbrick, an immensely rich landowner and prodigious collector. Part of Pugin's brief was to incorporate fifteenth, sixteenth and seventeenth-century woodcarvings into the rooms. This he did with triumphant success, as in the little Oak Room where the fireplace is a medieval choir-stall beneath a canopied Rococo overmantel. His own designs are intermingled with the rest of the carvings but it is difficult to know which is which.

The King's Room next door has Pugin's panelling, great gothic doors and twenty-seven full-length royal and other portraits, thought to be by Edmund Thomas Parris, standing round in an arched frieze.

Pugin was only twenty-four years old when he was called in to remodel the house, and it was his first independent commission as an architect. He had trained under his father, showing an astonishing precociousness; he was asked to design the furniture for Windsor Castle when he was only fifteen. He was to develop a passionate love for the gothic, for its way of revealing rather than concealing the bones of the building. To him it was Christian architecture, whereas the classical was pagan.

The bare bones were revealed at Scarisbrick, with the roofs rising and falling with each room and wing. A great clock tower was built and to give the clock-face more prominence, Pugin built it into a projecting storey with a two tier roof. It was gothic, with a startling resemblance to Big Ben, which would be built in

The exterior

Noah's Ark in the Oak Room

The King's Room

London a few years later.

Sir Charles Barry, the architect for the Houses of Parliament, was assisted by Pugin but would never give him the credit for the clock's design or admit to the source of his inspiration. He went only so far as to say that, in the midst of their struggling for a design, 'an example was remembered', which needed 'endless modifications'. Not according to Gladstone, who remarked on the strong similarity when he visited Scarisbrick in 1867.

The clock tower was pulled down in the 1860s and the soaring 170-foot tower was built in its stead.

Charles Scarisbrick had led the life of a recluse in his splendidly opulent surroundings. He would refuse to see anyone, even those who worked for him, and one man, coming on business from London, had to return south after a day's pleading, without an interview.

He never married, although he had a mistress in Germany. An unexpected source of gossip is Nathaniel Hawthorne who, when American Consul in Liverpool in 1857, overheard some talk of Charles Scarisbrick on the train: '. . . according to some reports, he kept a gambling house in Paris . . . He is a very eccentric and nervous man, and spends all his time in this secluded Hall, which stands in the midst of mosses and marshes, and sees nobody, not even his own steward.' Hawthorne had already walked past Scarisbrick the year before and had written that 'the country about Southport has as few charms as it is possible for any region to have.'

When Charles Scarisbrick died, he had left orders that his coffin was to be taken in a 'direct line' to the church: hedges had to be cut down, three ditches had to be filled in, he was carried over a wheat field and a cabbage field and through the gap in the presbytery wall that he had mysteriously ordered to be left open some years before.

THE TATTINGSTONE WONDER

Suffolk

THE TATTINGSTONE WONDER WAS BUILT IN 1761 BY THOMAS SQUIRE WHITE OF TATTINGSTONE PLACE, both as a pleasing ecclesiastical eyecatcher and also, it is said, to give people something to wonder at when they were so often wondering at nothing. His father had built the red brick Tattingstone Palace, as the house was called, some forty years before and laid out the gardens with an ornamental lake. (It has now been enlarged to the great Alton Water Reservoir.) His son was to leave his mark with this little 'church' on the horizon. Originally a row of three brick farmworkers' cottages, they were faced with flint and ashlar, gothicised and aggrandised with the three walls of a buttressed and crenellated tower.

Today it is one lofty dwelling, converted by Mr and Mrs Steven Solley in 1975. (Strangely enough, they also live only yards from Squire White's original family house in Hackney Wick.) It has been sensitively transformed and is much loved.

Hessie and Charles Smith, who now live in a modern bungalow in Tattingstone village, were the last occupants of the Wonder before its conversion. Hessie's father, George Porter, looked after the horses on the estate in the 1930s and 40s and Hessie can remember carrying buckets of water to the steam threshing machine. Her father had grown up in the Wonder as did his children and his grandchildren, and one of his great-grandchildren was born there. The family lived in the middle cottage; the Wards and the Bilners lived on either side. Mr Bilner's job was to clear the woods and the ditches.

There was no running water in the cottages; it all had to be drawn up from the well which still stands in the garden, as does part of the wash-house, a little square, red brick building which had a copper for each family and a tiny fireplace. There were three outside privies. 'You used to have to dress up in your big army overcoat,' laughs Charles, 'and reverse in, otherwise you were stuck for coming out. You couldn't turn round in them; if you did, you would bark the skin off your elbows and everything else on the bricks.'

When they first moved, Hessie was always putting on her coat and charging out into the garden.

They had a tin tub in front of the fire for years. There were three bedrooms with either the point of the gothic arch as a window or, at the back, a little square one which you had to kneel on the floor to look out of.

The house was modernised, 'if you can call it as such', in 1962 when one plug and two light sockets were installed in the only room downstairs, but they never had any water. The kitchen was twenty-two feet square. It had a brick floor which was so uneven that it dipped a foot or more in places, 'but you did not have to

buy rocking chairs, you sat on any chair and you could rock them. We hadn't fridges or anything like that, they weren't about in those days and we used to have our meat safe which we would hang outside. We didn't have washing machines, just scrubbing boards and mangles.'

'It was hard work, real hard work,' says Hessie, 'but we survived it, didn't we? We did enjoy it, it was nice there, it really was.' 'That,' says Charles, 'is a matter of opinion!'

A kneeler, showing the Wonder in St Mary's Church, Tattingstone, made by Miss F. Tracy

TAYMOUTH

Perthshire

THE ANCIENT CASTLE OF BALLOCH IN PERTHSHIRE WAS GIVEN THE NAME TAYMOUTH WHEN IT WAS TRANS-formed into a classical and crowstepped pile by William Adam circa 1730, for the second Earl of Breadalbane or 'Old Rag' as he was called, about whom there were 'curious stories', according to Sir Walter Scott, 'but chiefly such as paper will not endure'.

The results of his building work, which included an urned porte-cochère and bartizans, showed a 'thorough inattention to every idea of beauty and taste', according to the landscape gardener William Gilpin. Taymouth was inherited by the third Earl in 1752; he built a number of curious lodges and follies in the park which still survive.

In 1797 the next Earl decided to rebuild Taymouth once again as a castle and embarked on a costly false start with the architect John Paterson. The foundation stone was laid in 1801 but, after four years of work, Lord Breadalbane changed his mind about both the site and the architect. He had already spent £12,000, but everything was demolished and John and Archibald Elliot, who were responsible for building so much of Edinburgh, were employed as the new architects in 1806.

They designed a stately and delicate gothic castle skirted with cloisters and with an eighty-foot high central staircase tower. The main rooms are on the first floor. Those on the ground, behind the cloisters, are low and dark, with a long vaulted hall down which you walk, quite unprepared for the sudden explosion of the soaring gothic stairwell. It was finished in 1807 but not gothicised for another two years, with the Earl getting dangerously close to commissioning a classical scheme from Sir John Soane. Francis Bernasconi, an Italian plasterer living in London, was finally chosen. He started work on 1 June 1809 and produced a glorious

The Banner Hall

The splendour of the drawing room ceiling

Mirror on the ceiling to prevent cheating at cards

The soaring gothic stairwell

essay in the gothic, with decorated and perpendicular arches rocketing up to the bursts of fan vaulting. Lord Breadalbane paid Bernasconi some £33,000 for all the work that he was to do on the house.

The second Marquis was a man of lavish tastes who employed James Gillespie Graham to remodel the west wing as well as the interior of Taymouth. Frederick Crace applied the decoration, and between them they produced rooms of intricate and brilliant richness. The ceilings of the breakfast and drawing rooms are gilded and painted, moulded and carved with knights, troubadors, arms and grotesques. Delicate stags sit under gothic canopies above the mirrors and every door. The library is encrusted with fantastic decoration and Bernasconi's ceiling, above the great pinnacled chapel of a fireplace, in the Banner Hall has been covered with the arms of the Scots clans.

Queen Victoria visited Taymouth in 1842, when 'a splendid body of Highlanders, armed with Lochaber axes and halberts, lined the grand entrance'.

A grand fête with bagpipes, dancing and fireworks and a ball in the Banner Hall were enjoyed, as well as a splendid dinner, with 'Mr Wilson the celebrated vocalist' singing such airs as 'Pibroch o' Donnuil Dhu'. The Queen visited the dairy built of quartz and Prince Albert shot capercaillie, casting a cloud over the lyrical descriptions of the visit to Taymouth and its vast estate. It was said that Lord Breadalbane could travel a hundred miles in a straight line on his own land.

The castle was a hotel from the 1890s until 1939 when the War Department took it over as a hospital for Polish Officers. After the war it was empty until 1960, when it became a school for American children for five years. It is now owned by Taymouth Castle Hotel Ltd and surrounded by a golf club.

The Keeper's Lodge

The Architectural Library

Table, chair and balcony designed round the sun

CHARLES JENCKS IS AN EXPONENT OF POST MODERNISM. HE METICULOUSLY APPLIED IT TO HIS HOUSE IN LONDON, an 1840s stock brick and stucco building, when he remodelled it in the early 1980s.

The exterior was rather severe and straightforward before its metamorphosis; now it soars off in all directions. Two slender 'sunburst' chimneys, with stagger motifs at their base, the Egyptian and Greek symbol of earth, rise out of the curving roof. There is a steel grid balcony and pediment to signify Post Modernism, stuccoed balconies jut into open arches, symbolising a face, and the same form appears in the arched windows.

After you have grasped the double handles, one each side of the front door to represent hands, you begin your parade through the 'seasons' of the house. From Spring, you walk into Summer, with the golden glow of wood 'to recall the rays of the sun'. The chairs are fashioned from fibreboard, which can be hewn into sharp forms, layered and moulded with ease, giving architectural forms to the eye as well as comfort to the body. On account of its bursting back, Jencks has called it the 'Sun Chair'. The table too was designed round the sun, with an inlaid central circle of orange wood and with nine planets painted on each side of the legs, rising up to another solar symbol of a shiny wooden ball. Its rays, 'Apollo's arrows from afar', are cut into the balcony and zig zag all over the ceiling.

'Summer' blends into 'Indian Summer' in the kitchen. In real and *trompe l'oeil* marble, there are columns and panels that both conceal and enhance the workings of a kitchen and a frieze of spoons that marches round above the kitchen sink: 'Spoonglyphs – to symbolise the pleasures of eating.'

Spiralling up the centre of the house is the 'Solar Stair' (its structure was designed by Terry Farrell and David

The Summer Room

Model of Tuscan Temple in Moonwell

The kitchen with spoonglyphs

The staircase, one step for every week of the year

The Solar Stair, with rails representing the sun, earth and moon

French), which has fifty-two steps, one for every week of the year, each one cast with seven sides, one for every day of the week, so that there are 365 surfaces, one for every day of the year. With four steps to a month, each is represented by signs of the zodiac etched on circles of mirror, covering the holes left by the scaffolding support. Three rails revolve down the stairs, representing the sun, earth and moon. From below, they whirl up to the light and a glass dome; from above they swirl down to the dark and a black mosaic by Eduardo Paolozzi.

The walls of the staircase bulge into 'The Architectural Library', with a window in the form of Jencks's stylised 'face', revealing the layers that are built into the staircase cylinder: stucco, brick, reinforced concrete, brick and stucco. The bookcase 'buildings' are designed in appropriate styles: pyramidal forms tower over volumes of Egyptian architecture, gables spike up over works on the nineteenth century and 'Post Modern is indicated by anthropomorphism, a current preoccupation.' Four plain blocks of twentieth-century 'bookscrapers' have been banished round a corner.

Upstairs, the Moonwell, with its crescent, half and full moons, was designed in collaboration with Terry Farrell, Simon Sturgis, Ilanca Catacuzino and Charles Jencks's wife Maggie Keswick. It is on an axis with the Solar Stair and, according to Jencks in his chapter on 'The Thematic House' in *Symbolic Architecture*, this mirrored and glass shaft perfectly illustrates his thesis for the house: '. . . unified by Free-Style Classicism and the symbolic programme . . . Ornament, lighting, space, artwork and colour have all been directed towards the common theme not because we are moon worshippers – or I hope lunatics – but because symbolic architecture fulfills a desire.'

ST. MARY'S HOSPITAL

Chichester

I T IS DIFFICULT TO BELIEVE THE SIGHT THAT MEETS YOUR EYES WHEN YOU WALK THROUGH THE DOOR OF ST. MARY'S Hospital. You are undoubtedly in a church, with the nave sweeping up to the altar, but there are little houses either side of the aisle, with brick chimney breasts soaring up through the timbered roof.

These are almshouses in what is a remarkable survival of a medieval hospital that was founded in the late 1100s near the Market Cross in Chichester. It moved to its present site in 1269 and the building that stands today was begun in about 1290.

There are eight houses, two to each chimney breast, built by the Custos (the resident Canon), Dr Henry Edes, in the 1680s. Originally one large room, today each has a bedroom, sitting room and a bathroom as well as a kitchen which is built behind the nineteenth-century wooden railing that runs the full length of the aisle. To give solace to the soul as well as to the body, the building has every appearance of a church, with the delicate screen leading into a chapel at the head of the nave. One of the conditions of living in St. Mary's is that chapel must be attended every weekday morning, for a short service starting at 9.30 am. In 1905 it was decided to segregate the sexes and today eight ladies live in these overwhelmingly cosy houses. In 1987 their average age was approximately eighty-four, with Miss Gill aged ninety-two and Miss Eade aged ninety-four. St. Mary's is unique in that, of the few medieval hospitals that survive (there is one in Lübeck and another at Beaune), none has proper little houses built into its walls. Originally beds would have stood the full length of the hall, which might then have been partitioned off, but never more than that.

Transcripts of documents from these early days were made for the Dean and Chapter in 1775, with the form

of admission for 'the brothers and sisters who served God in the Hospital'. 'If any one seeks the Hospital of St. Mary . . . let the Prior consider whether he is a person of good conversation, of honest life and character, likely to be useful in serving or labouring for the poor . . . the Prior should first point out to him the poverty of the house, the poorness of the food, the gravity of the obedience, and the heavy duties . . . If a brother, under the instigation of the devil, fall into immorality, out of which scandal arises . . . or if he strike and wound the brethren or clients, or commit any other grievous irregularity, then, if he prove incorrigible, he must be punished severely, and removed from the society like a diseased sheep . . . if the brother shall have a quarrel with a brother and noise and riot, let him then fast for seven days, on Wednesdays and Fridays, on bread and water, and sit at the bottom of a table and without a napkin.' All the gifts and endowments were

recorded: 'To God and to His blessed mother Mary, and to the Hospital founded in the City of Chichester to receive weak and infirm poor people, of a faggot of eight squares of sticks, so as to warm the poor people who have been received into the said House.'

In 1528 Dean William Fleshmonger wrote a new set of statutes. Where previously people had been able to shelter for the night at St. Mary's, to have their feet washed and 'as far as possible, their necessities attended to', it was now stipulated that there should be five residents 'worn down by old age and infirmity', each with a room of his own. They were instructed to lead chaste and sober lives and to pray hourly for the Church, the King and Queen and the citizens of Chichester.

St. Mary's Hospital survived the Commonwealth, with Cromwell even giving it financial support, and it has survived intact to this day.

THE EGYPTIAN HOUSE

Penzance

A SURVIVOR OF ENGLAND'S 'EGYPTIAN REVIVAL' AT ITS MOST DARING AND DASHING, THE EGYPTIAN House was built circa 1835. It is an almost exact copy of the 1812 Egyptian Hall that stood in Piccadilly, but fractionally less flamboyant. In London, the window frames were besprinkled with hieroglyphs and two naked figures of Isis and Osiris stood over the lotus columns; in Penzance, two draped female busts are on plinths.

P. F. Robinson was the architect for the Egyptian Hall and, as its Cornish progeny is so startlingly similar, it would seem to have been built by the same hand. It is known that Robinson worked in the vicinity, on Trelissick House, near Truro. The architect John Foulston has also been credited with this dazzling out-of-scale and out-of-place Egyptian palace. He practised in Plymouth, and built an Egyptian library in Devonport in 1823, although his building was more restrained, with no figures at all on the façade. His partner George Wightwick wrote a description of him out driving in Plymouth. 'The vehicle which served him as a gig . . . was built in the form of an antique *biga*, or war-chariot; with a seat furtively smuggled into the service of comfort, though he ascended it from behind with true classical orthodoxy and looked (as far as his true English face and costume allowed) like Ictinus of the Parthenon, "out for a lark".'

Piranesi had brought the Egyptian Style to architectural attention in the mid-eighteenth century and it was to become popular in England during the next fifty years. James Playfair and Joseph Gandy, influenced by antiquities in Rome, were using Egyptian motifs by the 1790s, with Gandy even suggesting pyramids for 'pigs, poultry and their keepers'. Thomas Hope popularised this taste with an elegant Egyptian room in his house in

London, which he opened to a discerning public in 1804. With Napoleon's campaigns in Egypt, the fashion was fuelled in all directions. Robert Southey wrote complaining of the craze in 1807: 'At present, as the soldiers from Egypt have brought home with them broken limbs and ophthalmia, they carry an arm in a sling or walk the streets with a green shade over their eyes. Everything must now be Egyptian: the ladies wear crocodile ornaments, and you sit upon a sphinx in a room hung round with mummies, and the long black lean-armed long-nosed hieroglyphical men, who are enough to make the children afraid to go to bed. The very shopboards must be metamorphosed into the mode, and painted in Eygptian letters, which as the Egyptians had no letters, you will doubtless conceive must be curious . . . the strokes of equal thickness, so that those that should be thin look as if they had elephantiasis.' The Rosetta stone, which broke the hieroglyphic code, was not to be deciphered for another fifteen years.

It was thought to be a barbaric and barbarous style by many and few of its buildings have remained intact today. The sober and severe Temple Mills in Marshall Street, Leeds is still standing, designed by Bonomi in 1838 and based on the Temple at Edfu. Sheep were kept grazing on its roof, handily convenient for the flax-spinning mill but there were occasional and terrible disasters as they crashed through one of the sixty-six glass domes onto the machinery below.

The Egyptian Hall in London (demolished in 1904) and the Egyptian House in Penzance, which was beauti-fully restored by the Landmark Trust in 1968, were inspired by the Temple of Hat-hor at Dendra. With their great coved cornices, winged disks and lotus columns, all blazing out from their elegantly tapering façades, they personified the Regency dream of Egypt.

THE TREE HOUSE
Pitchford Hall, Shropshire

IT IS SAID THAT THE TREE HOUSE AT PITCH-FORD HALL IS THE OLDEST IN THE WORLD, HAVING SURVIVED FOR THREE HUNDRED years, perching in the branches of the same lime tree. It was built in the seventeenth century, classicised and gothicised in the eighteenth and, in 1980, was restored to its original timbered exterior whilst retaining its enchanting gothick windows and interior.

It is a miniature version of the multi-gabled and timber framed Pitchford Hall, a building which is thought to have been started either in 1500 or 1550. There are no firm clues as to when the tree house was built. The Ottley family, who bought the land in 1473 and lived at Pitchford for thirteen generations, might well have built it for Adam Ottley as a miniature replica of the hall which he had inherited in 1695, when he was only ten years old. A painting on wood, signed by John Boiven and dated 1714, shows the little house on stilts, with the young Indian lime tree growing up beneath it.

In the mid-eighteenth century Adam Ottley, who was meticulously careful with his money, accounting for everything down to 'Sheeps head for dogs, 2d', flamboyantly decorated the little building with exquisite 'rococo-gothick' plasterwork. Bows tie up gothic arches on the coved cornice; cluster columns fill each corner; a mask is surrounded by sun rays on the ceiling; and undulating ogee arches wave over the door and windows. In W. Cowan's pen and ink drawing of 1854, these glories can be glimpsed through the window, with the stuccoed exterior framed by long and short quoins. It is probable that the plasterwork was done by Thomas Farnolls Pritchard, a Shrewsbury architect recently rediscovered who, with a group of carvers, was responsible for gothickary all over Shropshire and Herefordshire, including elaborate work at Croft Castle and on some thirty-five other houses as

well as four church monuments.

Before the last two Ottleys died in 1807, they appointed Charles Jenkinson, afterwards third Earl of Liverpool, as their heir. He was the future Queen's godfather and Victoria came to see Pitchford and the tree house in 1832, when she was thirteen years old. The hall appeared to her as a huge and curious black and white striped cottage and she visited 'the little house in the tree' after church.

The next occupants of Pitchford (it has never been sold to this day) were Lord Liverpool's daughter, Lady Louisa Cotes, and her husband John, the High Sheriff of Shropshire, a popular figure who, according to his obituary in the *New Monthly Magazine* in 1874, 'had the happy talent & the amiable disposition of rendering himself agreeable to all ranks & classes of men; frank, affable, & friendly in his deportment, he sought conversation with the beggar as well as the Peer, & on both he never failed to impress some pleasing recollection. – "I say, my honest fellow!" was his usual mode of challenging to a conversation any peasant on the road, & there was not a peasant for miles around who would not have sacrificed his life, to serve "Squire Cotes".'

In the first half of this century, Pitchford was to experience the startling occupancy of Lady Sibyl Grant who, Salopian gossip insisted, lived in the tree house, occasionally meeting her husband on the lawn for coffee. She was unable to bear the sound of water to the east of the hall and had been terrified of haunting from the graveyard to the north, and so she had moved out, to live in either the tree house or the orangery. James Lees-Milne, in his published diaries, *Prophesying Peace*, describes meeting her in 1944: 'I saw a fat, dumpy figure waddling and supporting herself with a tall stick. She wore a long, blue coat down to her calves. One foot had on a stocking, the other was bare. On her head was an

The tree house in 1854 and 1988

orange bonnet, draped with an orange scarf which floated down to her ankles. She had orange hair kept in place by a wide-meshed blue net. She took great care to shield her extraordinary face, extraordinary because, though the skin is beautiful, the shape is absolutely round and the lips are the vividest orange I have ever beheld. She looks like a clairvoyant preserved in ecto-plasm . . . She had sprained her ankle – hence the one bare leg – and made me pour a solution of Ponds Extract over it out of a heavy lead Marie Antoinette watering can.' On another visit he wrote of her being in her 'delicious tree house'.

In 1976, Mr and Mrs Oliver Colthurst, who live at Pitchford today, embarked on a grand programme of restoration of the little building. It took four years to perfect and was opened by the Lord Mayor of London on 24 May 1980.

The name Pitchford comes from a curious bitumen spring that flourished in 'a poor man's yard' in the village. In the early seventeenth century Marmaduke Rawdon of York described the phenomenon: 'Thir is in well four little hooles, about halfe a yard diep, out of which there comes little lumps of pitch, but that which is at the tope of the well is softish, and swimes upon the water like tarr, but being skimd together itt incorpo-rates, and is knead together like soft wax and becomes hard.' As late as the twentieth century it is recorded that 40lb of pitch was 'scumm'd off'.

The eighteenth-century plasterwork interior

THERE IS NO MORE EXOTIC HOUSE IN THE BRITISH ISLES THAN 8 ADDISON ROAD IN WEST LONDON, BUILT BY Halsey Ricardo for Sir Ernest Debenham in 1906. It glistens from top to toe, outside with brilliant blue and green glazed brickwork and cream Carrara ware, inside with tiles, mosaic, marble and rare woods.

Despite its startlingly curious appearance, Ricardo's design was based on the soundest of principles – to build in materials impervious to the corroding effects of the city atmosphere and to define the architectural lines with colour rather than with bulging embellishment – and a luscious architectural extravaganza was to emerge.

After the first shock of seeing the house rearing out of the trees near Holland Park, you are surprised still further by having to march along a forty-foot long covered way to the front door. Elegantly roofed at its entrance, with wrought iron gates by the Birmingham Guild of Handicrafts, it is a gleaming stretch, from end to end, of peacock blue and dark green tiles, with panels of flowers, vases and stylised peacocks, all by William de Morgan. Ricardo's name and the date of the house are on a panel of cypress and pomegranate trees in a Tuscan landscape.

Despite all this, you are still not prepared for the glories to come, which quite startle you out of your wits on opening the door into the front hall. It is Sir Ernest Debenham's masterstroke: sheer walls of brilliant turquoise blue tiles rise up to marble balconies piercing the pendentives of an immense mosaic dome. Ricardo had wanted to leave this white, but Sir Ernest, inspired by Ravenna, had commissioned Gaetano Meo to design these glittering scenes. The balconies, with openwork Byzantine patterns and their elaborate pillar capitals, were all designed by George Jack, who made furniture

The Byzantine Hall

Brass, glass, enamel and ceramic detail in the hall

The exterior in the open-air breakfast room

for Morris and Company for some years. The whole house was a hive of industry for the Arts and Crafts Movement: William Aumonier carved the stair newell post, E. S. Prior made all the coloured glass panels and the Birmingham Guild of Handicrafts made the door furniture and light fittings, all of them brass inlaid with enamel. Ernest Gimson designed the library ceiling and, of course, there was William de Morgan, whose tiles cover almost every flat surface of the house: there are flying rats and owls pouncing on mice in the bathrooms, peacocks stand beneath trees in the passages and sixty glinting lustre ships sail round a bedroom fireplace. There are twenty-eight tiled fireplaces in the house, six of them in the bathrooms and no two are alike.

Often in a multitude of patterns, with the mantelshelves, surrounds and hearths in three different marbles, some are like great town halls; others are tiny and modest. Many of the tiles were part of an order for the Czar's yacht 'Livadia', which was torpedoed in the First World War. 'The interior of the house is both dignified and charming', wrote an alarmed estate agent in 1954, when the remainder of the lease was sold for only £6,000. (Sir Ernest had never managed to buy the land on which he built his £50,000 house.) In 1964 it was taken over by the Richmond Fellowship, the excellent organisation for community mental health, when, according to the founder and director Elly Jansen, it was still only half the price of any comparable lease. 'It was not a fashionable house.' How the illuminati would love its glitter today!

Technologically too the house was a triumph: there was an alarming central vacuum system run by a great motor in the basement, with filtered nozzles suctioning in the filth throughout the house and, even more extraordinary, a telephone connected to the theatre for

Gaetano Meo's mosaics in the Byzantine Hall

live performances. Beatrice, wife of the youngest child Martin, who was born in the house, can remember the delights of living there during the war: 'Although it was empty Henry the butler was there, very light on his feet in white tennis shoes.' She was an ambulance driver in Tunbridge Wells and would come to London every Friday 'on one of those sinister unlit trains with no corridor and a cigarette light burning in the corner', to be welcomed 'with lovely china tea and toast' into this glowing temple. 'It was quite creepy during the bombing though, but the house felt so safe and strong; a five hundred pounder fell in the garden and we didn't feel a thing. The caretaker, who always wore an Anthony Eden hat, made a potato patch out of the enormous hole that it had made.'

Sir Ernest's wife had great difficulty in moving into the house with its sheer ceramic walls and its violent decoration, where an inch of her own decorative schemes would have been an intrusion. 'The men had expressed themselves like mad all over the place.' But all eight children were brought up there, every one a 'lively, ebullient and original individual'. Their mosaic portraits, with their mother's and father's, blaze out today amidst the signs of the zodiac, Jason and his crop of warriors sprung from teeth, Ulysses, Orpheus and other Greek heroes. A quotation from the Odyssey marches round their feet. A charming detail is how the children helped to create it all; Gaetano Meo had set them to work, each with a little calico bag of chippings.

All this took place in a country-like wilderness: the gardens of this urban palace rolled into its own field which, filled with cows, stretched over to Holland Park.

THE JUNGLE

Lincolnshire

THE GNARLED AND SCRUNCHED-UP FAÇADE OF THE JUNGLE AT EAGLE WAS BUILT BY THOMAS LOVELY FOR Samuel Russell Collett in about 1820. With its purple and blackened overburnt bricks and its gothic door and windows, it was a picturesque face for a plain, red brick farmhouse and a dramatic backdrop for the menagerie of creatures that roamed free on the lawns. After going through years of neglect, it has been resuscitated and turned into a magnificent modern mansion by Audrey and Dennis Houlston.

A Major General Loft visited the house in 1826 and wrote a description of the 'very singular but tasty and handsome residence' with its 'grotesque but not inelegant appearance . . . Several Deer of different Kinds are kept here, the American Axis which has produced a breed from the Does; there are also several very fine Kangaroos, a Male & a Female Buffalo (I think) and their young Calf, all these are running loose together . . . In some of the neighbouring Inclosures Mr Collett has several foreign cows . . . In the house are many good apartments.'

Today it has got electrifyingly 'good apartments', with an immense swimming pool, over which the stars of the galaxy are flashing, in different colours, through a marbelised formica ceiling. A mosaic of the house stands at the end of the pool, lit by red, blue, pink and yellow lights. A circular bar, in two-tone brown formica with bamboo panels, juts out into the recreation area behind the jacuzzi. The sauna is lined with beige, cream and silver honeycombed foil and the solarium with turquoise and silver marbelised foil. Upstairs, the pink carpeted snooker room has a glass wall to look down on the bathers.

The Jungle was bought by the Houlstons in 1965. They demolished the farmhouse, retaining only its

extraordinary façade. This three-foot deep burnt-brick castle stood for a moment alone in the middle of the fields. The entrance front and the main bulk of the building (there are two towers behind and nine square, projecting bays) were finished by 1976; the swimming pool wing was built in 1984.

The rooms have been designed on a splendid scale and have been splendidly decorated: The sixty by forty-foot drawing room, in old rose and chartreuse green, has a pink marble and punched green leather bar, surrounded by gilded furniture inset with circular enamel plaques. One bedroom is hung with padded peach velvet, another is furnished with the Chinese Collection from the nearby town of Newark, the result of an astonishing service by which you can have whole suites of furniture made and painted in Hong Kong, to match precisely the material you have chosen. One bathroom is lined with panels of pink, cream and silver foil and pink and green wool, all draped with festoons of silk flowers; another sports red and black striped tiles with firework explosions of cream dots. The whole house has been attacked with verve and spirit.

A galaxy of stars shine down on the swimming pool

The paint-encrusted walls of the kitchen and attic

Eyes lead up to the attic

SIXTY-THREE HORNSEY ROAD IS AN ORDINARY TERRACED HOUSE THAT WAS ATTACKED WITH AN ORIGINALITY THAT quite takes your breath away. From the hall to the attic it bulges, twists and curves with brilliant colours and curious forms. Mrs Daisy Rogers is responsible for it all and she is genuinely unaware that there is anything out of the ordinary. 'Anyone can paint walls; I wanted to make it look pretty you see. I had no leanings towards the artistic, it was just a matter of splashing on the paint, finding shells and going out and getting another chandelier or two, to smash up for the "jewels" which you embed in plaster of Paris. Did I suggest that they may look like a heap of jewels from Araby?' These are her explanations for the terrifying decorative explosion and, when asked how she came to use such a mixture of colours, she says that the local paint shop was closing down and that she bought about 200 tins of whatever was going at the time.

Before she moved to Hornsey she had led a particularly conventional life with her first husband, a scientist 'who got cleverer and cleverer and cleverer'. They lived in a large house with a great deal of polished furniture. 'I really worked hard, so that you could eat off the floor, but who wants to? One day I painted the imitation leather chairs pale blue and stippled them with red, and I removed the oak mantelpiece and replaced it with a lot of shells embedded in blue plaster. I also painted the piano pale blue, after cutting off its knees and lid to make into a coffee table. Well none of those things went down well. He did not like it, not one bit.'

She met her second husband, 'Rogie', in 1961, 'on April 6th at twenty minutes to four and we eloped in June.' He already had the shop on the ground floor of 63 Hornsey Road and they moved into the house in 1966. It was painted dark brown and pale green throughout and she set to work on the stairs immediately, starting at the top, painting enormous eyes in Siamese pink and kingfisher blue which swirled down to shell and 'jewel'-encrusted mirrors and masks embedded in the walls. On the last flight, there is a transparent plastic woman, her head filled with dried teazles, who looms out over pink fans and octopuses, one of them a portrait of 'Rogie'.

A mask of her first husband was built into the Blue Grotto under the kitchen table. 'I thought it would be a suitable place for him. It's not that I had anything against him, it is just that he was bad-tempered and dull. I think if people are that, they deserve to lose you.'

The kitchen was gouged out with grottos and it is the most startling room in the house. Daisy draped two of the walls with calico, steeped in plaster of Paris, over screwed-up newspaper to bulge out the folds, and flung on paint mixed with Polyfilla, so that the thick drips of intermingling hues slithered down, over the swathes, to the floor.

There are vast landscaped railways both in the sitting room and in the attics (one is presided over by another mask of her first husband) with all the houses made by Daisy, meticulously to scale and from life.

Soon it will all be gone; Daisy is moving to a small new house. 'I am going to have a fridge and a washing machine and a proper gas stove and a stainless steel sink, you know, nice things.'

Daisy Rogers' first husband under the kitchen table

Daisy Rogers' first husband painted as an octopus on the staircase

HARLAXTON

Lincolnshire

HARLAXTON, AND ESPECIALLY ITS GRAND STAIRCASE, IS OF A STYLE AND SIZE THAT DEFIES COMPARISON WITH any other house in England. Part neo-Elizabethan and Jacobean, part baroque, and with a great deal of individual flair and fancy, it was built by a Mr Gregory Gregory for himself and himself alone between 1832 and 1851. He was helped by three architects, Anthony Salvin, Edward Blore and William Burn, but it is said that the last two only 'whispered in his ear' as he thundered on with his overwhelming creation.

He never married, he disliked his heir and he never entertained; he channelled all his passions and energies into the building of this vast and sensational palace. 'The grandeur of it is such, and such is the tardiness of its progress, that it is about as much as he will do to live till its completion,' wrote Charles Greville who went to Harlaxton in 1838. He was right; after 'embodying himself in his edifice' for over twenty years, Gregory Gregory was to live in it for only three, enjoying a bachelor existence, with only one bath and over 120 rooms. He had one startling and unique convenience: a train to bring in the wood and coal for the fires, that trundled along a brick viaduct, built specially and raising the tracks to the level of the hill into which the back of the house was built.

The exterior of Harlaxton is like a great golden town at the end of the drive: towers, pinnacles, gables and ornamental chimneys, strapwork cresting, cupolas and spires, all soar out of the great mass of buildings. With the baroque gate piers curving round and the Elizabethan turrets shooting up, all with such verve and spirit, this massive and hefty pile seems to be lively and light with movement, entirely filling your range of vision as you approach.

Inside, the staircase has a baroque splendour that is

The plaster drapes and the ropes and tassles gathered up by babies in front of the mirrored 'windows' on the staircase

Through the arch at the end of the long straight drive, the pile of Harlaxton

Soaring up the stairwell past the swags and swirls to Father Time unfurling a plan of the house

unequalled anywhere in the country, with its swooping and swirling of swags of fruit, ropes, tassels and drapes with hundreds of cherubs nestling in their folds. Mer-babies with giant shells decorate the walls, surging up to 'heaven', a bright blue painted sky with two figures of Time. Both have real scythes, one with a medallion in relief of Gregory Gregory, the other unfurling the plans of Harlaxton.

In 1837 there was a roof-raising ceremony with Greg-ory Gregory giving a dinner for all who had worked on the house. Two thirds of it had been built, 'enough', according to a local report, 'to show that, when per-fected, it will reflect honour on the arts of this country, and hand down the name of its founder with disting-uished éclat to a remote posterity.' A flag was hoisted up the central tower, 'unfolding itself in the bosom of the heavens', and Mr Weare, the Clerk of Works, roared a speech from a newly built turret: '"May prosperity of every kind attend the projector of this noble dwelling! May he live to complete it, and enjoy possession of the same for many many happy years to come!" This was followed by nine cheers and one more.' A procession then marched to the feast in the village, with the workers carrying the tools of their trade; the labourers with mortar hods, the masons with squares, levels and compasses and the bricklayers with plumb rules and trowels, all decorated with ribbons and evergreens. Guns were fired, songs were sung and 'recitations and sentiments gave a variety and effect to this most gratify-ing commemoration'.

Harlaxton was threatened with demolition in 1935 but it was rescued by another extraordinary figure, a Mrs Violet Van de Elst who had amassed a fortune from Shavex, the first brushless shaving cream.

The house is now the British campus of the American University of Evansville.

The roaring fire, with shelves on either side of the chimney piece, and the stained glass dome

SPRINGFIELD ROAD

Brighton

Davıd Mayhew's curious little house was designed to show what can be built with cement and chicken wire: 'To explore ways of building small structures that would be both durable and compatible with a natural landscape . . . It is well tested and used in conventional building . . . It is in one piece and therefore immensely strong . . . It can be altered or repaired with ease . . . It can be fully insulated . . . It is economic and it can be decorated in a variety of ways.'

These are his claims and they are all true. The building, twisted into the forms that took his fancy, cost only £80 in materials and it is a proper little house, with a pleasing and mellow finish. Inside it is like a Greek church, with the sun, when shining through the stained glass of the dome and windows, aflame on the rough whitewashed walls.

It is a delight to be in, cosy, strange and beautiful.

Gothic arches rise up at either end, one enclosing the chimney breast with its tiny blazing fire, the other framing the window, a bird perch and the washing bowl fed by rainwater. The dome gives an added dimension of space, as does the panel of looking glass and, with the walls swooping about in all directions, with no straight or constricting lines, there is not the slightest sensation of claustrophobia, despite the fact that the room measures only seven foot by three foot. David Mayhew often sleeps in the house, on the cement bench/bed that runs the full length of the little white room.

He built a small gothic church in 1984 and realised that the already established method of ferro-cement construction could be adapted to any shape or form. He believed, too, that it could be capable of elegance and set out to prove this by making imitation vine-entwined Jacobean frames entirely of wire and cement. It worked,

The exterior and interior of the stained glass bay window, the bed, and the washbasin filled with flowers

and they have all the appearance of elaborately carved wood. He has made urns, chairs, tables, lamps and candelabra, as well as an imitation rockery with a waterfall and a small 'Norman' castle 'which could be scaled up for children'. His fireplace, a creature's head with an open yawning mouth, is in daily use, as are his washbasins, with water pouring from lion head spouts.

David Mayhew realises only too well that the eccentricity of the house 'is taken a little too far . . . for a serious construction, it would be larger and more dignified.' He has prepared a drawing of a cottage which cannot be faulted: a small 'stone' house with a gothic door and windows, a bay at either end and barley sugar twist chimneys. As an added bonus, it can be mounted on wheels, '. . . to get round planning regulations . . . if you have to move it, you can, five tons is nothing on a trailer'.

His new plan is to construct houses in sections, each measuring four foot by four foot. They will be made up of two layers of cement, with polystyrene 'sandwiched' between them for better insulation. Each will have a tube built into it which can then be threaded onto a skeleton of scaffolding where they will be cemented together. Two have been finished, one above the other; inside are dark 'Jacobean oak' walls with pillars, heraldic capitals and a 'rough oak' sill beneath gothic windows. Massive looking 'stone' moss-clad walls are on the outside, ornamented with lions' heads, columns and figures.

David Mayhew sees it 'as a way of building when once again the emphasis is placed on the character and skill of the individual . . . more akin to sculpture than mere mechanical process'.

The Bavarian splendour rising out of a moat in Surrey

A MOCK TUDOR MANSION OF 1834 LURKS UNDER THE RHENISH GOTHIC SPLENDOUR OF HORSLEY TOWERS. The first Earl of Lovelace bought the brick and timber pile built by Charles Barry in 1840 and, over the next thirty years, was to transform it into this flint and brick candle-snuffer castle.

A keen amateur architect and engineer, Lord Lovelace was responsible for the entire building programme which, after the house was finished, extended to rebuilding the estate village of East Horsley, all in the same fantastical flint and polychrome brick. Many were appalled by his fanciful extravagances. In the *Gardeners' Chronicle* of 1886 'H.E.' particularly criticised the towers, 'one of which is circular and surrounded by *mâchicoulis* . . . one cannot help asking why towers are required for this purpose, since a policeman would perform the duty better.' Arthur J. Munby wrote of the horror he felt in 1864 when visiting the village: 'Many of these old houses are being pulled down by Lord Lovelace, who builds instead of them places of astounding eccentricity, barbarous to the last degree.'

One of Lovelace's first architectural acts at East Horsley Place (soon to be ennobled with 'Towers'), was to build a vast banqueting hall with 'steam heated' arched trusses supporting the roof. The main beams had been bent to the required curve after being exposed to the steam for five hours in a 'stout air-tight plank chest', and then the smaller roll and cavetto mouldings were treated in the same way. He gave a lecture on the process to the Institute of Civil Engineers and won their professional acclaim. Isambard Kingdom Brunel was not able to conceive 'how the advantages of such a construction could be at all questioned'; he preferred it to any system that he had used and had 'seldom seen so simple and useful a roof'.

The view as you emerge from the underground drive

The dazzle of the cloisters

After a lapse of some seven years and inspiring travelling abroad, Lord Lovelace returned to building in Surrey with almost lunatic quirkiness. He gouged out the back drive through tunnels under the garden; he built the extraordinary Bavarian tower, flooding the park so as to make it rise out of a moat; and he designed brilliantly colourful horseshoe cloisters as well as twenty-four horseshoe bridges. The cloisters, with royal blue, scarlet and chrome yellow stained glass windows and multi-coloured brick vaulting, lead you into the chapel, a journey of some three steps within the house and of some five, cold minutes by this roundabout route. They are at first floor level, surrounding the back courtyard and rearing up over the back drive as it sweeps out of the tunnel. As they curve, you drive under them again, as well as another archway, to reach the front of the house.

Engineering was very much a part of Lord Lovelace's architectural adventures; as well as relishing the triumph of all the arches and tunnels, he enjoyed revealing the bleaker bones of its technology. Iron rods span the cloisters and ridge the brick vaulting, in one case with a whooshing parallelogram, and the entrance to the chapel is supported by drainpipes. He was concerned that the new possibilities of 'mechanical excellence' might supersede 'artistic feeling', and set out to dispel such worries at Horsley Towers with a wealth of idiosyncratic work in flint and moulded brick to such a high standard of excellence that he won the medal for brickmaking at the Crystal Palace in 1851.

The Earl was Lord Byron's son-in-law; he had married the studious and brilliant Ada in 1835. But she was to die in 1852, before the grander extravagances of Horsley Towers were under way.

The church towers
out of the vicarage

MORWENSTOW VICARAGE

Cornwall

A SINGULARLY ROMANTIC FIGURE, ROBERT STEPHEN HAWKER, THE POET PARSON WHO CONSIDERED HIS contemporary Englishman to be nothing but a 'dextrous blacksmith' and all of England to have deteriorated to the state of 'a kind of railway station', built the Vicarage at Morwenstow in 1837.

He came to his parish, 'my fatal gift of Morwenstow', in 1834 and until 1875 was to live a lonely and flamboyantly unconventional life with his Cornish flock – 'a mixed multitude of smugglers, wreckers and dissenters of various hue'.

He chose the site of his house where he had seen sheep shelter from a storm and where 'the only objects perceptible from my two fronts will be the church and the sea', and after finding a plan whereby 'frugality may be exercised without the appearance of poverty' in T. F. Hunt's *Designs for Parsonage Houses*, he set to building,

with his own spirited additions. Five of the six chimneys are models of the church towers where he had lived: Stratton, Whitstone, North Tammerton and two in Oxford. The sixth, he wrote, 'perplexed me very much, till I bethought me of my mother's tomb; and there it is, in its exact shape and dimensions'.

He restored the church, insisting that the roof be covered with oak shingles, 'tiles of wood – the material of the Ark and of the Cross', with disastrous results, and he removed the bottom panel of the pulpit, deeming it essential that the congregation should be able to see the priest's feet, as well as his dogs, who often sat with him during the sermon. He had all the box pews removed and when one farmer refused to disband his great house-like shelter, Hawker himself destroyed it with an axe. There was a tiny door in the screen that led to the pulpit which could only be squeezed through with the greatest difficulty, but he refused to enlarge it. 'Don't you see that this typifies the camel going through the eye of a needle?' It could only be passed through backwards on leaving the pulpit, and one of Hawker's delights was to release a trapped visiting preacher with the words 'It is the strait and narrow way and few there be to find it.'

He was a considerable poet. Tennyson admitted that 'Hawker has beaten me on my own ground' with his 'Quest for the Sangraal', and his poetical nature stood him in alarmingly picturesque stead. His clothes were extraordinary: a long claret-coloured tail coat; a blue fisherman's jersey (to show he was 'a fisher of men'), knitted with a red cross to mark the entrance of the centurion's spear; hessian boots up to his knees; and either a 'Wide-awake Beaver' or a pink fez on his head. 'I don't make myself look like a waiter out-of-place, or an unemployed undertaker.' With his long grey hair flying, followed by his nine cats, he would process up the aisle, always ankle deep in herbs – southernwood, thyme, wormwood and sweet marjoram. After pacing about behind the screen orating half in Latin, half in English, he would suddenly appear, to prostrate himself on the ground in front of the altar.

Shipwrecks were the curse of his life at Morwenstow, 'with the breakers roaring after their prey, to seek their meat from God' smashing ships against the great boulders beneath his house. He would stand helpless as bodies, either alive or dead, were hurled onto the rocks around him, but was always there, either to save lives or bear the corpses in mournful procession up the cliffs to conduct a proper Christian burial. His was the first church in England to hold a Harvest Festival.

THE PAGODA

Blackheath

THE PAGODA AT BLACKHEATH IS A RARITY, ONE OF THE RELATIVELY FEW SURVIVORS OF THE EXOTIC CHINESE style that dazzled England in the eighteenth and nineteenth centuries.

The ruin of a tiered pagoda for monkeys still stands at Culzean in Ayr; two elaborate little garden temples are about to be restored at Biddulph Grange in Cheshire; and a Chinese fishing temple survives at Alresford in Hampshire, but by the very nature of their fancy fragility, the little buildings are sadly few and far between.

With its ornate forms decorating anything from a hog house to a bridge over the Thames to a hermit's cell with thatch in the 'Chinese taste', the Chinese style was often the butt of merriment and mockery: '. . . all is Chinese,' wrote John Shebbeare in the mid-eighteenth century; 'the walls are covered with Chinese paper filled with figures which resemble nothing of God's creation,

and which a prudent nation would prohibit for the sake of pregnant women . . . so excessive is the love of Chinese architecture become, that at present foxhunters would be sorry to break a leg in pursuing their sport in leaping any gate that was not made in the Eastern taste of little bits of wood standing in all directions.'

The style reached the peak of its popularity in the 1750s and Sir William Chambers gave it architectural respectability with the publication of his *Designs of Chinese Buildings*, for which Dr Johnson, 'much pleased' with the contents, wrote a foreword. Within months Chambers was commissioned to build the Pagoda at Kew.

It is thought that this curious building in Blackheath was designed as a summer house in the early 1760s by George Brudenell, fourth Earl of Cardigan, who lived at nearby Montague House from 1751. It passed to his daughter Elizabeth, who married the third Duke of

Buccleuch, 'whose name was never mentioned with-out praises by the rich and benedictions by the poor,' according to his friend Sir Walter Scott. *The Dictionary of National Biography* records him as having 'imitated James V of Scotland in paying visits in disguise to the cots of his humbler dependents who always profited thereby'.

At the turn of the century, the Pagoda was taken over by Princess Caroline, the Princess of Wales, who opened a school in the house and cultivated the garden with the 'judicious combination of the useful and the agreeable'. The German educationalist, Joachim Heinrich Campe, was pleased to note it all down in his diary of 1803: 'I was charmed with the neat borders of flowers . . . and was doubly rejoiced to find them so small; because, as the Princess remarked, too much room ought not to be taken from the useful vegetables, merely for the purpose of pleasing the eye . . . I was transported with the elegance, taste, and convenience displayed in the Pavilion.' This is a happier picture than the one eighteen years later of Princess Caroline, in sumptuous state regalia, hammering at the doors of Westminster Abbey in a vain attempt to be allowed into her own coronation. George IV had not been permitted to divorce her eight months before and had his rich revenge with this public humiliation.

In 1821 the Pagoda was lived in by Frances, Countess of Dartmouth, who had borne the Earl five sons and nine daughters. Between 1832 and 1841, her second son, the Revd Henry Legge, Vicar of Lewisham, lived there, calling it 'Chinese Cottage'.

After a variety of owners, it was sold to the London County Council in 1951, to be a children's home. In 1986 it was used to house refugees from Sri Lanka. The Pagoda is now owned by the London Borough of Lewisham.

WITLEY PARK

Surrey

WHITAKER WRIGHT'S UNDER-WATER SMOKING ROOM IS ONE OF THE ODDEST ROOMS IN England. Once lushly comfortable with semi-circular padded sofas, a mosaic floor and palm trees, it was part of a labyrinthine network of ramps, tunnels and chambers, some decorated in the Oriental style, that were built both underwater and underground in the late 1890s and early 1900s.

Between 400 and 500 men were employed to work day-in and day-out for seven years on a grand 'improvement of nature' throughout the whole estate. Hills were levelled and refashioned elsewhere and old lakes were filled in and three new ones created with boat houses and temples and statuary galore. One fountain, a dolphin's head from Italy, was so enormous that the railways refused to transport it north from Southampton. Whitaker Wright sent a traction engine to haul it

home and when it came to a bridge that it could not pass under, ordered that the road be lowered until it could.

In 1903, the *Royal Magazine* published an account of all the building activities, under the scrutiny of 'a sombre silent man in black from the City of London . . . He strode about his park, carrying a great oak stick, superintending. Everywhere he saw chances of improvement. "We will have a great lake here," he said in effect, with a wave of his oak staff, "this hill blocks the view – take it away. Cut down this wood. Here we will have a grotto. An Italian fountain would look well here. But first have a wall built, ten feet high all round," and he waved his stick with an all embracing sweep. It was a standing joke of the workmen to say, every time they saw that oak stick waving: "There goes another hundred pounds!"'

The underwater smoking room alone was said to have cost him £20,000. 'It is a wonderful place – a fairy

A fish swims roun *underwater smok* *room*

palace,' wrote the same observer. 'In summer it is delightfully cool – in winter, delightfully warm . . . Outside the clear crystal glass is a curtain of green water – deep, beautiful green at the bottom, fading away to the palest, faintest green at the top, where the little white wavelets ripple. Goldfish come and press their faces against the glass, peering at you with strange magnified eyes. On summer nights one looks through the green water at the stars and the moon, which appear extraordinarily bright and large, for they are magnified quite ten times by the curved glass and the water.'

Whitaker Wright was an extraordinarily rich man; by the time he was thirty-one he had lost two and made three fortunes through mining speculation in America and New Mexico. He went from strength to strength, controlling mines in Australia, Canada and America and a multitude of finance companies in England, but in 1900 they crashed, dragging numerous small investors with them and Wright himself who was prosecuted for having manipulated the accounts and sentenced to seven years' imprisonment for fraud. After accusations of excessive 'window dressing' of the balance sheets and the loss of some £8,000,000, he killed himself with cyanide within minutes of the verdict.

The technological feat of building this 400-foot long tunnel under a lake, leading to an eighty-foot high underwater conservatory, must be attributed to the Controller of the Chicago Tramways, Charles Tyson Yerkes who, with Sir Robert Perks, was to buy up and develop London's underground system from the 1890s. They built two tunnels under the Thames and it is known that Yerkes often visited Whitaker Wright. He too was prosecuted for embezzlement and imprisoned. His motto was not exactly one to inspire confidence: 'Buy old junk, fix it up a little and unload it on another fellow.'

CRAVEN COTTAGE, LONDON

Craven Cottage in Fulham was built by Lady Craven, later the Margravine of Anspach, in the 1780s. She was a dramatist, composer of musical farces and authoress of such works as *Modern Anecdotes of the Family of Kinvervankotsprakengatchdern, a Tale for Christmas*.

In 1805 the cottage was leased to Walsh Porter, an art dealer in the Prince Regent's circle, 'whose refined taste stood alone' according to some, but was 'grotesque and ridiculous' according to others. He needed somewhere to show off both his person and his pictures and employed Thomas Hopper to help with the transformation of the rustic retreat.

It was glorious, with every exotic taste in full flower. In the Egyptian hall every aspect of that new style of decoration was crammed into one room. Four slender palms, with carved drooping foliage, and eight immense columns covered with hieroglyphics rose up as high as the ceiling. Serpents supported the chairs and tables and there was a huge bronze woman draping a

curtain of imitation tiger skin over a bronze camel. The windows were all tapered, as were the doors, with massive and intricately carved surrounds.

The house was burnt down in 1888 and Fulham football field is now on the exact site of all these glories. In 1986 the land was threatened with redevelopment and it was wonderfully strange and very funny to see the protesting club supporters standing, in their hundreds, roaring with one voice: 'WE WANT CRAVEN COTTAGE . . . SAVE OUR CRAVEN COTTAGE . . . CRAVEN COTTAGE . . . CRAVEN COTTAGE'

LOUDON'S COTTAGE IN THE 'INDIAN STYLE'

John Claudius Loudon designed a labourer's house in the 'Indian Style' in his *Cottage, Farm and Villa Architecture* which was published in 1836, 'to improve the dwellings of the great mass of society, in the temperate regions of both hemispheres'.

The little Eastern building is shown with an ornate and smoking chimney pot in the middle of a domed roof. It is surrounded by a verandah and decorated with a quantity of

'appropriate Indian forms'. It was thought to be suitable for 'a man and his wife, without children' and was to have two rooms: a kitchen/eating room/washroom/sitting room and a bedroom, as well as a tiny lumber room and a pantry. A privy was to be built at one end of the garden and a well at the other. The total cost was estimated at £207.18s.

Any person 'under usual size', such as the cobbler whose case is cited, could arrange a bed in the lumber room, although this was considered to be 'making shift, a thing not to be recommended in any book written with a view to human improvement'. For people of 'ordinary size', the lumber room was still

possible, with a built-in box for feet that jutted out into the next room, where it was disguised as a chest of drawers.

Loudon suggested that this tiny temple be built on a 'flattened summit of a knoll', where it could be seen from all sides, 'forming as it were an architectural plinth . . . it will not be denied that the result will be somewhat dignified'.

Loudon's book is full of such descriptive and architectural delights, with a villa in the 'Italian Style', of the same style and dimensions as the Pitti Palace, a 'caprice' of a Chinese gateway and a terracotta chimney with angels blowing smoke out of their mouths – all created 'to diffuse among mankind, generally, a taste for architectural comforts and beauties.'

HALFPENNY'S BANQUETING HOUSE

The architects and brothers William and John Halfpenny produced an enchanting little pattern book in 1750 entitled *Rural Architecture in The Chinese Taste*, with plans for a banqueting house that looked as if it was aflame with all its decoration. Every inch and angle was embellished, and dragons with forked tongues flew off the edges of the roof. Obviously the workmanship was all of the highest quality, as the point of the designs was to 'attempt to rescue those agreeable Decorations from the many bad consequences usually attending such structures'. It is suggested that the ornate building should be 'agreeably situated on a Grand Amphitheatre of green slopes, or on a Terras'.

ROBERT LUGAR'S
ARCHITECTURAL SKETCHES

'In composing Architectural Designs for Dwellings it is not necessary the artist be trammelled by the cold rules of the school; some scope should be allowed to taste and fancy.' So wrote Robert Lugar in his *Architectural Sketches for Cottages, Rural Dwellings and Villas in Grecian, Gothic and Fancy Styles*, published in 1815. With three of his buildings he kept wildly to his word, with 'taste and fancy' raging and rampaging over a cottage, a villa and a summer house.

For his 'Ornamented Cottage and Ruins', even the ruins were to be built as part of the whole design. The idea to be conveyed was an abbey mutilated, and to show the cottage, as if dressed out of the remains, with rooms 'sufficient for a numerous and respectable family'.

The 'Villa in the Eastern Style' was acknowledged by him as having been taken from 'Mr Daniell's views of India'. It is described as being of only moderate expense, with 'curtailed' enrichments, and as ideally adapted 'to the conveniences of the English nobleman or gentleman'.

RICHARD BROWN'S
DOMESTIC ARCHITECTURE

Richard Brown published his book in 1841 'to excite desire for cultivating taste.' It is an enormous tome; inside are castellated and classical piles side by side with splendid Egyptian and Turkish pavilions, along with every other conceivable style of architecture – Swiss and Burmese, Florentine and Plantagenet, Anglo-Grecian and Morisco-Spanish, each shown in its natural setting. Obelisks tower out of the palm forests round 'An Egyptian Pavilion' and a pagoda soars up on Chinese crags behind 'A Chinese Residence'. All were suggestions for houses that could be built in England, Eastern and Oriental palaces that were to be domesticated into English life. But Brown's stern dictum, to marry the landscape with the house, was at odds with the exotic styles and all he could do was show them in their native environment.

The Egyptian Pavilion owes a great deal to the description of Medinal Abdoul's palace in Denon's *Travels in Egypt* of 1790, a book that had great influence on the Egyptian Revival in England. 'The Palatial Building in the Morisco-Spanish Style' was based on the deserted Moorish palace of the Alhambra, overlooking Granada. His

Chinese Residence is a symmetrical little villa flourishing with dragons and bells. The

Morisco-Spanish pavilion

A Chinese residence

additions of mid-Victorian chimney pots poking out of its pagoda-like roof are most unexpected and unsuitable.

Brown had not set out 'to make every gentleman his own architect', which he thought might well be 'prejudicial to the beauty, grandeur, and stability of our rural mansions'. He simply wanted to show that 'In forming new combinations, rich perspectives, scenic groupings, and pictorial union of architecture and landscape, there is ample scope for active imagination, taste and feeling.'

TIMOTHY LIGHTHOLER'S CHINESE LODGE

A Hog House and a Bog House flank the Chinese Lodge designed by Timothy Lightholer and illustrated in his *Gentleman and Farmer's Architect* of 1762. This was published when architectural pattern books were at the height of their popularity, when aspiring as well as established architects produced designs in a galaxy of styles.

Lightholer's book, with his suggestions for an assortment of gothic, classical and Chinese buildings, was one of the most

fanciful in this already fanciful field. He designed a Norman keep for a shepherd, to

stand at the head of a triangular and fortified sheepfold and 'to be built on a hill which seen from a genteel house forms an agreeable object'. There were classical cow sheds with arcaded wings, and garden walls in section, revealing the enormity of the pipes heating them up for choice fruits. Rarest of all and, sadly, unlikely to be realised, were his 'Façades to place in front of disagreeable objects': newly built 'ruins' complete with arrow slit windows, crumbling castellations and a gothic door, that were designed to disguise a farmhouse, barn and haystack.

His Chinese Lodge was almost as unrealistic. An agricultural building adorned with urns and oversize dragons with bells in their mouths, is not ideal.

SIR ISAAC NEWTON'S MAUSOLEUM

In 1834 a mausoleum was planned to encase Sir Isaac Newton's house. He had died over 100 years earlier, in 1727, when he had been buried in Westminster Abbey. It was now proposed that his home, in St. Martin's Street, Westminster, where he spent the last seventeen years of his life, should be preserved in a forty-foot high, stepped stone pyramid, sliced off two thirds of the way up, with a vast stone globe perching on top. If it had been built it would have taken up the whole of the south side of Leicester Square.

When Sir Isaac Newton died, an inventory was drawn up of the house which gives a vivid picture of the life that was lived there, from the 'two old bedsteads and three old blankets' in the back garret to the sedan chair in the stables and his library of 1,896 books. This extraordinary document, seventeen feet of 'skins sewn together' and only five inches wide, was found in Somerset House nearly 200 years later by a Lieut-Col. R. de Villamil, 'Royal Engineers (Retired)', who wove it into a delightfully critical book, with a foreword by Einstein, *Newton: The Man*.

> Nature and Nature's laws, lay hid in night.
> God said, 'Let Newton be,' and all was light.

wrote Pope as an intended epitaph.

Newton himself was modest about his life: 'I do not know what I may appear to the world, but to myself I seem to have been only like a boy playing on the seashore, and diverting myself in now and then finding a smoother pebble or a prettier shell than ordinary, whilst the great ocean of truth lay all undiscovered before me.'

ACKNOWLEDGEMENTS

First and foremost to Francis Graham, many thanks are due. Also to the following: Celestria Alexander-Sinclair, Andrew Arrol, Julian and Isobel Bannerman, Mrs Beulah Barnes, Lady Browne, Lord Burnham, the Marquis and Marchioness of Bute, Jim Carter, James Cartland, Mrs Ursula Colahan, Dr and Mrs Bruce Cole, Caroline and Oliver Colthurst, Mrs Julia Croft-Murray, Beatrice Debenham, Anne Dickson, Mr Dunn, David Evered, Mrs Eyles, Christopher Gibbs, Harry Graham, the late Sylvia Grant-Dalton, the Principal of Harlaxton College, Huckleberry Harrod, Simon Harwood, Mary Hesketh and the late Roger Hesketh, Miles Hildyard, the Very Reverend Robert Holtby, Dean of Chichester, Audrey and Dennis Houlston, Derek Hudson, Pat Hughes, Ralph Hyde, the Earl of Iveagh, the Trustees of the Edward James Foundation, Elly Jansen of the Richmond Fellowship, Charles and Maggie Jencks, Steven Johnson, Richard Kirkman, the London Library, Rod Malcolm, Frank Mann, Colin Mantripp, Sharon Martin, David Mayhew, Josie Montgomery, James Neidpath, Justine Oliver, John Outram, Graham Ovenden, Protocol, Niel Rhind, the RIBA Library, Ian Ritchie, Daisy Rogers, David Rowbotham, Michael and Elizabeth Sandford, Kuldip Sandhu, John Simpson, Charles and Hessie Smith, Ian and Jan Snowball of Group 3, Mr and Mrs Stephen Solley, Julian and Sarah Spicer, Ansie de Swaardt, Charles and Jessica Thomas, Susanna Thomas, Graham Tongue, Mrs Ursula Tudor-Perkins, Brian Webb, the Earl of Wemyss, Lucia Whitehead.

BIBLIOGRAPHY

ALDEN, JOHN R., *A History of the American Revolution*. London, 1969.

ALEXANDER, MICHAEL AND ANAND, SUSHILA, *Queen Victoria's Maharajah*. London, 1980.

BARING-GOULD, S., *The Vicar of Morwenstow*.

BECKFORD, WILLIAM, *Vathek*. 1786.

BOYNTON, LINDSAY, 'Luke Lightfoot' – from *Furniture History*, Volume II. 1966.

BRENDON, PIERS, *Hawker of Morwenstow*. London, 1975.

BYLES, C. E., *The Life and Letters of R. S. Hawker, Vicar of Morwenstow*. London, 1905.

CHANNON, SIR HENRY, *'Chips' – The Diaries of Sir Henry Channon*. Edited by Robert Rhodes James. London, 1967.

CONNOR, PATRICK, *Oriental Architecture in the West*. London, 1979.

CROCKER, T. C., *Walk From Fulham to London*. London, 1860.

CROOK, JOHN MORDAUNT AND PORT, M. H., *History of the King's Works*, Volume VI. HMSO, 1973.

CROOK, JOHN MORDAUNT, *William Burges and the High Victorian Dream*. London, 1981.

CURL, JAMES STEVENS, *The Egyptian Revival*, London, 1982.

DALE, ANTONY, *The History and Architecture of Brighton*. Brighton, 1950.

FAULKNER, T., *History of Fulham*. London, 1850.

GOTCH, J. ALFRED, *A Complete Account of the Buildings Erected in Northamptonshire by Sir Thomas Tresham*. London and Northampton, 1883.

HAWTHORNE, NATHANIEL, *The English Notebooks*. Edited by Randall Stewart. New York, 1941.

HINKSON, PAMELA, *Seventy Years Young – Memoirs of Elizabeth, Countess of Fingall*. London, 1937.

HUDSON, DEREK, *The Story of Pitchford*.

ISHAM, SIR GYLES, 'Sir Thomas Tresham and His Buildings' – from *Northants Antiquarian Society Journal*. Northants, 1966.

JACKSON, PETER, *George Scharf's London*. London, 1987.

JAMES, EDWARD, *Swans Reflecting Elephants – My Early Years*. Edited by George Melly. London, 1982.

JENCKS, CHARLES, *Symbolic Architecture*. London, 1985.

JOHNSON, SAMUEL, *The Works of Samuel Johnson*. Oxford, 1825.

LANSDOWN, DR, *Recollections of the Late Mr Beckford*. Bath, 1983.

MACAULAY, JAMES, *The Gothic Revival 1745–1845*. Glasgow and London, 1975.

MAXWELL, THE RIGHT HONOURABLE SIR HERBERT, BART., M.P., F.R.S., ETC., *Evening Memories*. London, 1932. *The Honourable Sir Charles Murray K.C.B. A Memoir*. Edinburgh and London, 1975.

MILNE, JAMES LEES, *William Beckford*. Tisbury, 1976.

MUSGRAVE, CLIFFORD, *Life In Brighton*. London, 1970.

Peacock, Davie, *Perth, Its Annals and Its Archives*. Perth, 1849.

Rhind, Niel (Blackheath Society), *Transactions of the Greenwich and Lewisham Antiquarian Society*, Volume III, No 6. London, 1978.

Robinson, John Martin, *Georgian Model Farms*. Oxford, 1983.

Turner, Stephen (Surrey Archaeological Society), *William,*

Earl of Lovelace.

Verney, Lady Margaret Maria, (Editor) *Verney Letters of the Eighteenth Century from the MSS at Claydon House*. London, 1930.

Villamil, R. D., *Newton the Man*. London, 1931.

also, 'Lovelace' – *Surrey Archaeological Collections*, Volume 70. 'Inspiration of Egypt'. Brighton Museum, 1983.

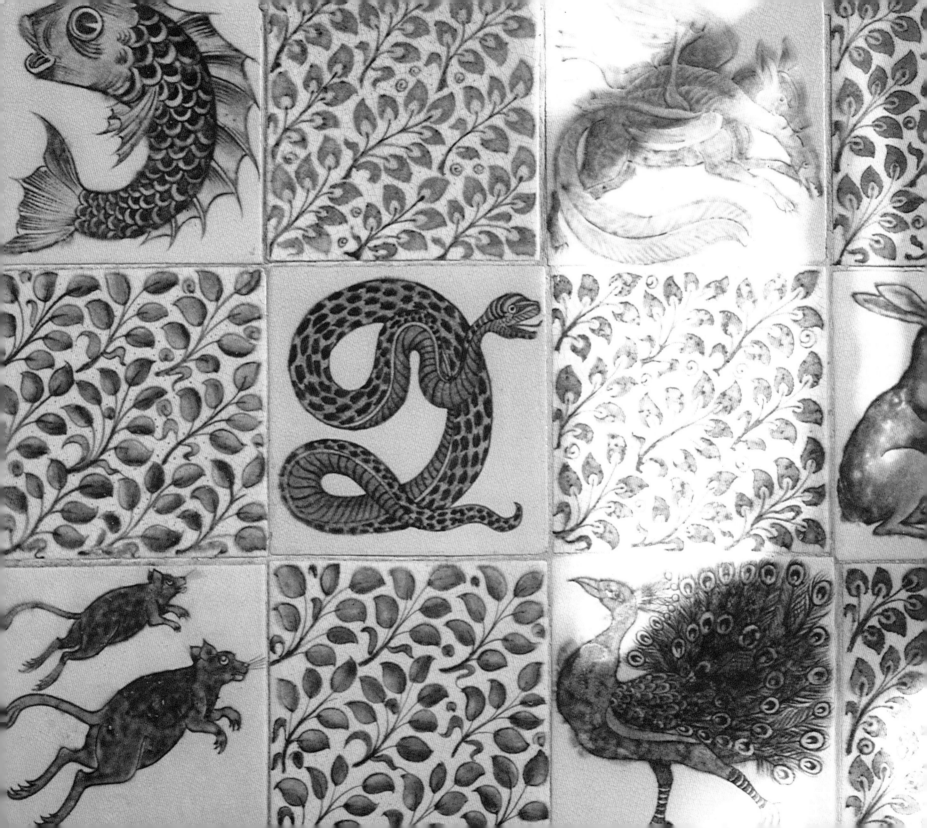